Praise for Bill Klatte

D1549002

"*Live-Away Dads*'s important message is that children need their fathers, even when they don't live with them. Klatte's book is a powerful tool for dads who want to get close and stay close to their kids. It provides men with the compassion, support, and straight-shooting advice they need to overcome the pain of separation and make a meaningful difference in their own lives and in the lives of their children."

—Michael Gurian, author of *A Fine Young Man* and *The Wonder of Boys*

"Klatte is on target. He knows the importance of dads to their children and details for dads who are separated from their children how to stay involved in their children's lives. *Live-Away Dads* can be read in an hour but its impact will benefit a father's relationship with his children for life."

—David Knox, Ph.D., divorce coach, http://www.divorcecoach.com and the author of *The Divorced Dad's Survival Book*

"*Live-Away Dads* is a very useful self-help book for fathers who do not live with their children. The book uses no academic jargon and does not refer to specific studies, yet Klatte's recommendations are entirely congruent with the best research literature in family sociology and child development. Indeed, the book is written in a direct, easy-to-read, conversational style.

"Klatte recommends building the best possible working relationship with the children's mother, and acting like a real father—not just a grown-up playmate—during parenting time. These are actions that will facilitate children's adjustment and development.

"This is not an angry book written by a maladjusted fathers' rights advocate. It is a responsible and sensible book that should be of use to all live-away dads who are struggling, against the odds, to maintain a close relationship with their children."

—Paul R. Amato, Ph.D., Department of Sociology, University of Nebraska–Lincoln

PENGUIN BOOKS
LIVE-AWAY DADS

William C. Klatte's twenty-six years as a social worker and psychotherapist included five years conducting custody studies and visitation mediation for county courts. He is currently the Fathering Outreach Specialist for The Parenting Network and a psychotherapist with Discovery and Recovery Clinic, an outpatient mental-health facility. He helped found the Milwaukee Men's Center, a nonprofit organization for divorced fathers, where he was a board member and men's divorce group facilitator. After his divorce in 1979, Bill Klatte became a live-away dad to his two daughters, then three and five years old. They are now grown and remain very close to their dad.

William C. Klatte

Live-Away
DADS

*Staying a Part of
Your Children's Lives
When They Aren't a Part
of Your Home*

PENGUIN BOOKS

PENGUIN BOOKS
Published by the Penguin Group
Penguin Putnam Inc., 375 Hudson Street,
New York, New York 10014, U.S.A.
Penguin Books Ltd, 27 Wrights Lane, London W8 5TZ, England
Penguin Books Australia Ltd. Ringwood, Victoria, Australia
Penguin Books Canada Ltd, 10 Alcorn Avenue,
Toronto, Ontario, Canada M4V 3B2
Penguin Books (N.Z.) Ltd, 182–190 Wairau Road,
Auckland 10, New Zealand

Penguin Books Ltd, Registered Offices:
Harmondsworth, Middlesex, England

First published in Penguin Books 1999

1 3 5 7 9 10 8 6 4 2

LIBRARY OF CONGRESS CATALOGING IN PUBLICATION DATA
Klatte, William C.
Live-away dads: staying a part of your children's lives when they
aren't a part of your home / William C. Klatte.
p. cm.
Includes index.
ISBN 0 14 02.7280 1
1. Absentee fathers. 2. Divorced fathers. 3. Fatherhood.
4. Father and child. I. Title.
HQ756.K52 1999
306.874′2—dc21   98–11684

Printed in the United States of America
Set in Janson Text

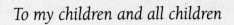

To my children and all children

ACKNOWLEDGMENTS

I would like to acknowledge all the dads whose stories and struggles are included here. They have often inspired me. I want to thank my brother, Owen Klatte, and his wife, Angie Glocka, for their ongoing support and encouragement through the years that I worked on this book. Thanks also to my daughters, Kyla Klatte and Chris Klatte, who have been not only an inspiration for this book, but encouraging supporters all along. All of you helped me keep writing when there was no way to know if anything would ever come from it. Thank you Pamela Prenger for your ideas and for caring.

I would also like to acknowledge my agent, Helane Hulburt, for her belief in this book, excellent suggestions, and hard work in finding an excellent publisher. Speaking of excellent publishers, thanks goes to the people at Penguin, particularly my editor, Kristine Puopolo, whose skill in suggesting changes that improved this book is very much appreciated.

Thanks, finally, to my parents, Jayne Klatte and Bill Klatte. Thanks mom for being such a stickler about English when I was growing up, and for caring and listening so well. Dad, you died too young, but you helped me appreciate how important dads are to kids, and you inspired me to do what I can to see that fathers remain an important part of their children's lives.

CONTENTS

IV. Fathering Your Children
155

V. Building a Network of Support
197

INTRODUCTION

Live-Away Dads: Staying a Part of Your Children's Lives When They Aren't a Part of Your Home is written for any father who does not live with his children because his relationship with their mother has ended. This includes divorced dads, separated dads, fathers who once lived with their children but never married their children's mothers, and dads who have never lived with their children. I call these fathers "live-away dads." They are biological fathers (or in some cases adoptive fathers or other men who have taken on an unusually close father-child relationship) whose children spend all, or the great majority of their time, living with their mothers. Live-away dads are no better or worse than fathers living with their children. They are just different. But the challenges faced by live-away dads are unique and can be overwhelmingly difficult.

There is a smaller group of women who live in situations similar to those of live-away dads, and even though this book is written specifically for men, I hope it will be of help to these "live-away moms" as well.

How many live-away dads are there? The 1990 census showed that, of sixteen million children under the age of eighteen in the United States living in one-parent homes, fourteen million lived with their mothers. In married-couple homes, another six and a half million children lived with their mother and a stepfather. That makes a total of over twenty million children living away from their dads. And the number increases as additional divorces create over a half million new live-away dads each year. Of the millions of stories that live-away dads could tell, the following one prompted me to write this book.

One day as a child-abuse investigator for the county department of social services, I received a referral regarding an eleven-year-old boy named Adam. Our department was called by his school because he had two small bruises on his neck and arm. When I interviewed Adam in school, he told me that the bruises were caused by his older sister hitting him. School personnel were not aware of any previous injuries to Adam, and his teacher felt that he was generally a well-adjusted child.

Adam's parents had been divorced for several years, and he now lived with his mother, Cheryl, and his sister, Jamie. I spoke with them next. Like Adam, they said that he and Jamie had gotten into an argument over something minor, and it had turned into a physical fight. Cheryl stated that she sometimes had difficulty controlling her son but that he was usually well behaved. Jamie and her mother acknowledged that physical fights were not a good way to handle arguments, and they agreed to work on better methods for dealing with conflicts in the future.

I then asked Cheryl what involvement Adam's dad had with his son and how I could contact him. She immediately pulled back. She told me he had no real interest in Adam and had hardly spoken to his son in months. She said that Adam never called his father and didn't miss him. She went on to say that her relationship with her former husband, Bob, was very strained, and communication between them was almost nonexistent. She implied that Bob would unfairly blame her for what had happened to Adam and wondered out loud what he could offer that would be of any help to her son.

In spite of Cheryl's resistance, I did get Bob's phone number and called him later that day. I wanted to know if he was aware of previous confrontations between Adam and his sister. I also felt that, as a parent, he had a right to know what had happened, and I doubted that other family members would tell him.

Bob was surprised to get my call. His previous contacts with courts or social workers during his divorce had been frustrating and painful. To him, it seemed that the legal system only saw him as a source of child support.

Bob spoke of great anger and mistrust between Cheryl and himself. He said he had struggled for years to have a good relationship with his children but that things were not working out.

According to Bob, contact had been fairly good until the divorce was final, but, soon after that, seeing Adam became more and more difficult because of the arguing between parents.

Bob acknowledged that he didn't call his son much, but said sadly that Adam sometimes didn't want to talk to him when he did call. Bob was also angry. Adam often wasn't ready to go when he arrived to pick him up. Sometimes Adam didn't seem to want to leave with him at all. Bob and Cheryl argued about when Bob's time with Adam started and ended. More than once Bob had arrived at Cheryl's house only to find that she had made other plans for their son.

Bob had other problems in his life too. He was current on his child-support payments, but it made living on his remaining income extremely difficult. He had a new wife and her children in his life, and those relationships were sometimes strained. His new wife was supportive of Bob, but combining the two separate families was not easy for her either.

Bob told me, "When my children were born I didn't expect to be a perfect father, but I did expect to be close to my kids all my life. But since the divorce, I've been spending less and less time with Adam." Driving to pick up Jamie and Adam for their time with him, he often felt sad and angry. Returning as a visitor to the home he once owned—and took such pride in—was very painful.

While married, Bob had sometimes taken for granted the times he had with his kids. He never thought he would some day have to schedule time with his own children or that every time he saw them he'd have to take a twenty-minute drive to do so. When married—even with competing school schedules, work commitments, hectic holidays, and the demands of daily life—Bob had been with his kids every day. Since the divorce, things had changed drastically. Missing his son and in constant conflict with Cheryl, Bob was dropping out.

I sensed that Bob did not recognize how important he was to his son, so I talked to him about it and repeatedly encouraged him to stay involved with Adam. I told him that although Adam might not understand why, he still needed his dad to be there for him.

Bob interpreted Adam's behavior as a rejection of him—but that's not what it was. Bob didn't understand that many children—whether they live in separated or intact families—are not good at communicating responsibly or understanding the sacrifices that parents make. Adam was reacting emotionally because of the divorce, his age, confusion about how to relate to his parents, and the conflict between his mom and dad. Adam was not rejecting Bob. He was just being a kid in the middle.

Two days later, Bob called to thank me for our conversation. Now I was surprised. I didn't get many calls thanking me for my social work. Bob said he was encouraged by our discussion and had phoned his son after we spoke. They had a good conversation and Bob was going to see him that weekend. He was feeling much more optimistic about their relationship. He was so happy and relieved after his talk with his son that he'd shed a tear when he'd gotten off the phone. Things seemed to be getting back on track.

A lot of tears are shed by strong and caring dads. I've shed tears of happiness myself, and, like other dads, I've also shed tears of sadness. After seven years of marriage and two children, my wife told me it was over. I moved out of the house. If married life had its ups and downs, divorce was often a living hell, especially in the beginning. We argued frequently. There was little trust or agreement on anything.

Separated from my children, rejected by the woman I loved, out of the house I spent so much time working on, alienated from some friends and family, saddled with heavy child support and feeling like a failure—I was lost. After our breakup, my former wife and I moved to different cities and ended up about one hundred miles apart. My daughters were barely three and five years old. I was often lonely, angry, and confused. There were many times when I felt like giving up.

Contact with my children was often painful because I missed them. Contact with their mother was painful because we argued a lot. We had lost so much. But I stayed in there for the long haul. I stayed committed to my children, and the rewards have been great.

My relationship with my daughters has blossomed. Every passing year brings us closer together.

Much of what I present to you in this book comes from my twenty-six years of experience as a social worker and psychotherapist—including five years as a county social worker conducting custody studies and parenting-time (visitation) mediation for the courts. This book also reflects my fourteen years of personal experience as a live-away dad.

Over the years, as I met more and more live-away dads personally and professionally, I ran into many who were angry, unhappy, and lonely. Some of their stories are here. Many are similar, and a few stand apart in their circumstances. But their emotional experiences, the frustrations these dads felt, and the questions they had seemed almost universal.

This book is written for any of the millions of live-away dads out there, whether they are trying to improve on a situation that is already satisfactory or are feeling trapped in their own private hell. Its purpose is to help dads stay dads—regardless of where they live, regardless of the odds against them.

I've written this book to be read from beginning to end, but you may decide to read just the parts that seem most relevant to you or to read and absorb it slowly over time. However you do it, keep it around as a reference, and return to it for guidance or support.

Every father is extremely important to his children. Just as every mother is. There are no exceptions. Although live-away parents have less time with their children, the quality of the time they do have together—and how they conduct themselves when they are not with their children—remains vital.

Unfortunately, too many live-away dads end up distancing themselves from their kids. Half of the fathers who get divorced and live away from their children gradually lose all contact with them. Not because they don't care. Not because they are selfish. But because of their own emotional pain, and because they are facing new and extremely difficult circumstances. Circumstances that, many times, they did not choose. Circumstances that would fluster any capable, loving, and effective parent—male or female.

Many dads drop out not because they don't care at all, but because they care too much. Research shows that many fathers who were less involved with their children before a divorce find that the opportunity to father on their own may actually enhance their father role. On the other hand, fathers who were highly attached and involved before the divorce often end up dropping out. They see their routine and time with their children being dramatically disrupted. Many fear even sharper decreases in access to their children and feel their strong and important father role being threatened. They experience grief with which they have difficulty coping.

Many are caring fathers like Bob, who are doing the best they can. But instead of attempting to understand and support live-away dads, many people focus only on the fathers who don't pay child support and write them off as "deadbeat dads." This is a term that angers me every time I see it in print. I even see "deadbeat parents," as if journalists are trying to be politically correct by slamming not just fathers but mothers as well. It's easy to condemn fathers from a distance. It is much harder to understand their plight or find legal and social ways to give them the opportunity to take on more meaningful fathering roles.

Nonpayment of child support is a serious problem, but namecalling is name-calling, and when derogatory labels are used so frequently for some live-away parents it affects all of them. Fathering from a distance is complex. There are many reasons why parents don't pay their full child support, and large numbers of separated fathers—and mothers—do keep current on financial obligations to their children. They pay child support in spite of the tremendous difficulty many have in seeing their children, in spite of the economic hardship it is to them (parents living with children are not the only ones with financial problems), and even though parents who receive child support can usually spend it on whatever they want with virtually no control or oversight by the courts.

Fathers often are treated unfairly by a court system that traditionally sees mothers as superior and proper parents—especially to younger children—and sees dads as financial providers. Moms are the cookbooks and dads are the checkbooks. After a divorce, courts routinely order that children live with just one parent, and 90 percent of the time it's with the mother. If a child is born out of wedlock, a dad doesn't have a ghost of a chance of having that child live with him regardless of who is the better parent.

This devastating inequity breeds anger and mistrust between parents and puts kids in the middle. It robs children of their fathers and places unfair burdens upon mothers. As a result, many parents act out their anger at the courts and each other while their relationships with their children become more and more distant.

Unfortunately, many fathers have not asked for—much less insisted upon—an equal role in parenting their children. Many of them did not have trusted male role models who showed them the importance of staying involved with their children, or how to father effectively. They haven't experienced involved and nurturing fathering from their own dads. Other fathers were pushed out of a parenting role by moms who didn't realize the importance of a father to his children and simply wanted him out of their lives.

But you can overcome these difficulties. Separation from your children's mother may be freeing. You now have the chance to parent *your* way when your kids are with you, and that can be exhilarating. You may or may not have chosen your current situation, but you can choose how you handle it, and many fathers use it to get closer to their kids.

Fortunately, ever-increasing numbers of fathers around the country are recognizing their importance to their children and fighting to be fully involved in parenting. The laws and prejudices that hold them back from full fathering are slowly changing. As that struggle for equality continues, it is hoped that this book will serve as a guide for dads to assure that their anger and pain do not alienate them from their children.

As they fight the fight for equality, live-away dads must continually look at their own behavior, work cooperatively with their children's mother, and be patient and loving with their kids. They must put their children first—as mothers must do. Unless these things are done, the fight will be for nothing.

The current legal system must be replaced by one in which children have more meaningful access to both parents. Dads who never married their children's mothers need a better opportunity to spend significant amounts of time with their children. In cases of divorce, children must be able to spend equal time—or nearly equal time—with both parents unless there is substantial evidence that sharing that time would clearly be more harmful to children than not sharing it. Additionally, any assessment of harm to children must take into account the harmful effects of limiting their access to both parents.

When equality in the judicial system is reached, fathers' outrage will be reduced. But it is no panacea, and it will not happen instantly. Geographic distance, severe parental conflict, and other conditions assure that, for all time, some dads—and moms—will live away from their children. There will always be a need for live-away parents, and separated parents sharing physical placement, to work on themselves to maintain close emotional relationships with their children.

Institutions and individuals need to focus first on helping families stay together. For parents who do split up, equity in the division of money and parental access to children must receive equal weight and attention. Only then can we expect more fathers to become fully emotionally and financially involved in the lives of their children.

Instead of spending so much time belittling "deadbeat dads," we need to recognize that nonpayment of child support is only one of several important problems faced by families that are split apart. Another extremely pressing problem is the large number of children being raised in this society without a close relationship with their fathers. All the money in the world will not solve that problem.

"Deadbeat dads" is just one term that I object to. I am also much opposed to the word "visitation." I consider it an antique word that has no place when talking about parenting. We *visit* Aunt Sally. We *visit* the zoo. But we *parent* our children. "Visitation" subtly relegates parents who do not live with their children to the inferior status of "visitor." This does a disservice to parents and children alike. Rather than "visitation," I refer to time parents spend with children as "parenting-time."

Words are extremely important. They reveal our beliefs, and conscious use of them can change our beliefs. Throughout this book I refer to the mother of my children as my "former wife" rather than "ex-wife." To me, "ex-wife" conveys a negative meaning. It rolls off my tongue, especially when I'm angry. "Former wife" is more neutral and doesn't come so easily. I have to stop myself and use it consciously, but by paying attention to the words I use, I cause myself to be less blaming. For years I was too angry at my children's mother to differentiate between "ex-wife" and "former wife." Actually, either of those would have been kind descriptors in the past. As time has passed, however, many of my wounds have healed, and I believe some of that is a result of the conscious way I speak about her.

Occasionally I hear people talk about dads "baby-sitting" their children. The American Heritage Dictionary defines a baby-sitter as "someone engaged to care for one or more children when the parents are not at home." In this book, "baby-sitter" and "parent" are never confused.

Legal terms such as "custodial parent" and "noncustodial parent" are confusing. What's more, "noncustodial" is a negative term, a constant reminder to millions of parents (primarily fathers) of what they don't have. To clear things up and avoid the negative, I refer to the parent who has his child living with him the lesser amount of time as the "live-away dad" (or live-away mom or live-away parent). I refer to the parent with whom the child lives the majority of the time as the "live-in mom" (or live-in dad or live-in parent). These terms reinforce *the importance of both adults as parents whether the children live with them or not.*

One more point of clarification: in this book, "separated" will refer not just to parents who are in the process of divorce but to all mothers and fathers living apart, whether they are divorced, legally separated, never married, or have never lived together.

To protect the privacy of people described in this book, names and identifying details of their stories have been changed, but their essential meanings have not. Stories and details about myself, however, have not been changed.

If you are looking for ways to become a happier, healthier, more effective father, this book might help. In it you will find ways to decrease conflict between you and your children's mother. You'll learn how to effectively deal with your pain and anger so you can enjoy life more. You'll find new ways to think about your relationship with your children and ways to enjoy your time with them even more. You will learn how and when to stand up for your children's needs—and effectively express your needs as well.

If you have a new partner in your life, you'll find ways to work more happily and cooperatively with her. She too has been thrust into a very difficult role. If you have started a new family, you will discover ways to balance the needs of that new family with the needs of your "live-away children."

You'll develop new ways to cope with your financial and property losses, and you will gain confidence in dealing with judges, social workers, lawyers, and other professionals. You'll hear what's worked for other fathers—and what can work for you.

Staying involved in your children's lives can be difficult, but you are not alone. You have more in common with other live-away dads than you might have thought. There are differences, to be sure, but they are usually on the surface. Some men get extremely angry in reaction to the ending of a relationship. Others become depressed. Some dads handle things beautifully. Some of us clam up, yet others can't stop talking. Some fathers handle stress well; some don't. A few don't seem to care at all about what happens. Others seem to care too much.

What do we have in common? Each one of us is important to our children. We all have the capacity to be great fathers whether we are living that way right now or not. We all have the ability to grow.

Great things happen when you put your children first and focus on improving yourself. As you do this, your relationship with your children will grow in ways that are hard to see right away, but they add up. If you commit yourself to your children for the long haul and think of their needs first, you lay the groundwork for loving and powerful relationships in the present and for the future. I've seen men do it. You can do it too.

PART I

Taking Care of Yourself

The greatest gift you can give your child is to take good care of yourself. The better you handle your life, the better your child's life will be because you'll make more healthy and loving decisions. Taking good care of yourself isn't selfish, it's practical. It's a way of loving your child.

You may be in great emotional pain. Possibly you've said or done things to your children or their mother that you'd like to take back. There may be many things you'd like to say but never have. Either way, you can't change the past. But you can change the future based on how you deal with life today.

Your relationship with your children and their mother has changed, but your life is not over. You decide how it goes now in spite of how often it may look like others control you. Ultimately, what you do to take care of yourself and make loving decisions has much more power than anything anyone else can do to you.

CHAPTER 1

Common Reactions to Breaking Up

"Man's main task in life is to give birth to himself."
—ERICH FROMM

On July 15, 1989, I was surprised by a noise at my door. I lived two and a half stories up, and that doorway opened onto a small airing porch with no outside stairs leading to it. I walked out on the porch to see a paperboy riding down the street on his bike and spied a rolled-up *Milwaukee Journal* at my feet. I had never had a newspaper thrown there in the four and a half years I lived at that address. I walked back into my flat and opened the paper. To my shock, I read the following headline on page one: "Fathers' rights activist held in fatal shooting of woman." This man had shot and killed his girlfriend in the bathroom of a bar.

The activist was not named, but I instantly knew who it was. He was a Milwaukee man I had met a few years earlier. He started an organization for divorced dads which grew quickly and, at one point, had several hundred paying members with chapters in over a dozen cities. He frequently spoke on the radio, was quoted in newspapers, and had appeared on the *Phil Donahue Show*.

His organization did things such as offer strategies for court cases, track legal changes, make law libraries available, and offer guidance on fighting custody and child-support orders. He believed that divorced men were treated unfairly by the courts, and he seemed driven to change the system. His organization was directed outward. Change the laws. Change child support. Change the former partner.

Around that time, I had been involved as a volunteer with several other men in an organization for divorced dads which I helped start. Our group took a different approach to helping live-away dads. We provided support groups, a fathers' support phone line, and events fathers could attend with their children. Our goal was to help men change themselves.

I had always thought that if that activist had looked more at his own behavior and less at the behavior of others, his energy and commitment could have done great good. Instead, he was convicted of first-degree reckless homicide while armed and sentenced to twenty-five years in prison.

This man's story is obviously an extreme example, but the point is that we are responsible for our actions, and we must act in ways that help our children and others, not harm them. This book is not about changing the courts or your children's mother. It is about taking control of your own life and making your personal relationship with your kids flourish. You have the power to do that.

Kids Need Both Parents

The anger and hurt that comes when a relationship ends can be so powerful that it affects our parenting. The breakup of any committed relationship is emotionally painful, but when there are children involved, it can be overwhelming. Because of those children, parents have legal, financial, emotional, moral, and spiritual connections to each other. They can't just go their separate ways. They are forced to deal with each other in spite of the pain.

Because children need both parents, fathers must search for ways to heal their own pain so that they can stay close to their children. There are many factors that influence our relationships with our

children: the courts, our childrens' mothers, finances, work schedules, and the distance between homes, to name just a few. But
more powerful than all these are our own actions because *they are the
only things we can truly control.* To take actions that help our children
and ourselves, we must look carefully at ourselves and heal our
wounds the best we can. Then we are on the right path to help our
children.

It can be extremely difficult to work cooperatively with your
children's mother after your breakup, but the enormity of that
struggle does not diminish its importance. Fair or not, she has a
tremendous influence over your relationship with your kids, and if
you work things out, you can get along better with her and get
closer to your kids. Things can be even better than they were when
you were together.

Every mom and dad I've ever talked to has agreed that children
are better off with two parents. After separation, however, their
opinions are often revised to include any parent but *that* parent.
Not after the way he acted. Not after what she did.

All men and women have strengths and weaknesses in parenting, but after they split up I frequently see them hold each other to
unrealistic standards. Separate parenting is a new experience for
both. Live-away parents don't know what it's like to live alone with
the children, and live-in parents don't know what it's like to live
without them.

Moms and dads intimately know the tough parts and easy
parts of their own situation, but they have not experienced what
the other parent goes through. They often make assumptions
about what their former partner "should" do, but, not having to
live it themselves, they are unfairly critical and harsh. At the
same time, they feel hurt or angry if the other parent doesn't appreciate the problems they have. They grow further and further
apart.

Live-in parents need to understand the value of the live-away
parent's involvement. They must support that involvement even
when it would be easier to do the opposite. At the same time, live-
away parents need to support the parent who lives with the kids

and stay consistently involved with their children even when they feel angry and unappreciated.

When parents are in conflict, I often see one parent use the behavior of the other parent as ammunition to get him or her out of their child's life rather than give support to do better. I understand the tendency to do that, but *it is not in a child's best interest.* Children are best served by two parents working together to overcome obstacles—not create them.

Suggesting that angry parents actually help each other may be too much to ask after a breakup, but it doesn't seem too much to ask that fathers and mothers at least not add to the difficulties of the other parent.

There are a very small number of situations in which it may be in children's best interest to temporarily take them away from a live-in parent or place restrictions on the time or conduct of a live-away parent. There are even cases of severe abuse or long-term abandonment in which either parent's contact with a child may have to be terminated permanently. But these are exceptions, and any decisions about limiting parental contact must consider the extreme importance of both parents to their children and must look closely at the role that both parents played in the problems that have occurred.

Dads Often Have Similar Reactions to a Breakup

The activist I mentioned at the beginning of this chapter had an extreme reaction to his relationship problems. Although few of us will react that strongly, it often takes great self-restraint to channel our emotions effectively. Our powerful responses grow out of loneliness, loss of control over our lives, separation from our kids, feared loss of our father roles, and material losses. For men, our response often comes in the form of anger.

Many of us have been taught all our lives—by parents, friends, employers, coaches, commanding officers, and societal rules in general—to react with drive and force when things don't go well.

For some of us those messages were clear and direct. For others they were more subtle and unconscious. Either way, when push comes to shove—we push and shove.

As a group member, and later a facilitator of divorce support groups, I have come to know many live-away dads. Many of these fathers had not wanted the split and were looking for ways to deal with their loss. For most of them, no matter how bad things had become in the marriage or how many times divorce was threatened, it was a shock to them when their wives told them for the last time, "It's over."

Parents who decide to end their relationships with their spouses or partners, as painful and difficult as that decision may be, have at least one thing going for them—control of the decision to end it. As a result, they are often more emotionally prepared for the separation. The person left behind feels he or she has no control. Abandoned. Rejected. A failure. A breakup is bad enough. Being left by a partner implies something worse—that the smart one got out by leaving the bad one behind. This is hardly true, of course, but it often feels that way to the person left behind.

A dad's initial reaction to a breakup and separation from his kids can produce some very strong feelings. Among the many fathers I've known, several responses to separation were common. The good news is that these were usually short-term reactions, and most men moved beyond them rather quickly. If, in the following pages, you recognize any reactions that you are going through or have gone through, realize that you are not alone. And that things do get better.

Loss of weight

Weight loss is often an immediate reaction to the ending of a relationship. Many dads lose twenty, thirty, forty pounds, or more. They have no interest in food. They are so emotionally wrung out that they can barely eat. Lack of appetite is often a symptom of depression, and depression is a common reaction to the ending of a relationship.

Fortunately, this reaction is usually short-term, and all the dads I've known have eventually gotten better. Usually within several weeks their appetites came back, and they began eating normally again.

Move into a crummy apartment

Dads who lived with their children's mothers before the separation often move immediately into the cheapest, smallest, most run-down apartments they can find. They may be handicapped in finding a good place because they do not have close male friends they can go to for help, and money is tight, but many behave as if they don't deserve anything nice or even reasonable. They seem to be punishing themselves for failing.

These dads do eventually move into better places, not just a place that costs more but an apartment or home that they want to be in. A place where they feel comfortable, not just a place to survive.

Give away everything out of guilt

Some dads blame themselves for the separation, and, in their shock, they exaggerate their own faults and minimize their partners'. Out of guilt, they give their former partners the house, the furniture, the best car, and excessive child support. They ask for nothing. As a result, they give up more financial resources and access to their children than is healthy for them, their former spouses, or their kids because, as time goes on, their children's mothers come to expect these unreasonably unequal arrangements.

Unless these dads are later able to work cooperatively with their children's mothers, they find themselves either in continual power struggles or stuck in an unfair situation. Both results only serve to worsen the conflict between them. Fortunately, these problems often diminish as time goes on and dads accumulate new possessions. They often lessen because changing circumstances in the lives of the children and parents require ongoing adjustments.

Depression

Many men react to separation with great depression. Some are suicidal. Their whole world has changed in an instant. It seems that everything they have worked for is taken from them. They no longer take pleasure in anything they do. They avoid people. They can't sleep. Some can't work or only do so by force of will. At the other extreme, some have so much excess anxiety and energy that they can't sit still.

In spite of these difficulties, the vast majority eventually overcome their sadness quite well. They find ways to cope with their problems. Time helps them heal. Some, especially those with serious depression, wisely seek professional counseling. Many dads grow from the entire experience. Even those who did not want their relationship to end eventually find out more about themselves and their strengths in the process.

Anger and blame

Many men react to the split with anger and blame. They fight with their children's mothers. They follow her. They swear and yell. Some get into physical fights with her or others. They slam doors, squeal tires, break windows, and get drunk. Others fume silently.

Had there been no children from the relationship, all of these dads might have just gotten on with their lives, but since children are involved, all that changed. Parents are forced to stay connected to someone they had rejected or who had rejected them. Trust is broken. Money conflicts begin. Anger and other strong emotional reactions surface. Many times those emotions focus on the children's mother or the courts. Sometimes it goes inward. Regardless of where it goes, people are hurt.

I'd like to say that all the dads I've met have gotten over their initial anger and pain, but a few haven't. Some have continued to blame and hate for as long as I've known them. Dads who were able to stop hating and get on with their lives were able to make the best of what they had. This is not to say that they always liked what they had, that it was easy, or that they didn't fight to change things they felt were unjust. It means they also recognized that they had a part in creating a life for their children and themselves and that they were responsible for making things better.

Frustration of not being understood

Many dads feel extreme frustration over not being understood by others. Their complaints to their children's mothers don't seem to get them anywhere. When they talk to others about their former partners, they often get weak responses. People who were neutral in the separation may listen, but, even then, dads may feel they are not really heard.

People who are angry at those moms for their own reasons seem to empathize more, but their reactions are still less extreme than the dads'. As much as these fathers want others to be as incensed as they are—it rarely happens. As troubled as others might be by what was going on, they can't know the details like these dads. They are not in their shoes. Their lives are less affected.

I am glad to say that many dads overcome this frustration. It happens when they realize that few people can fully appreciate what they are going through—except other men going through it themselves. They seek these men out at work, in their families, or in support groups with other live-away dads.

Underinvolvement or overinvolvement

Faced with the loss of their children, many dads become underinvolved or overinvolved in their children's lives. Extremely frustrated, they attack or withdraw. Some dads frantically try to control everything their children's mother does, and others silently pull away.

Although these reactions appear to be opposite, they have much in common. It is not unusual for dads who were initially overinvolved to withdraw later on when they see that they could not control what their children's moms did. So sometimes the initial attack was the beginning of, or a form of, withdrawal.

These actions are best seen as what they are—reactions to pain. Overinvolvement is an attempt to make things go a certain way, to provide predictability and a sense of stability. Underinvolvement is a way of gaining control of emotions. By saying to themselves, "I don't care," men try to minimize the pain and resentment within.

After my divorce, my attitude toward my former wife fluctuated frequently. Sometimes I wanted her to be happier. Sometimes I wanted to see her miserable. Often I told myself I didn't care one way or the other. But I always cared. Not in the way I cared for her when we were married or as I cared for my children, but rather as a person who had been such an important part of my life. I'd attempt to cope by saying that I didn't care, but that was really just a way of not feeling when things seemed overwhelming.

Extremes of emotion are common during and after divorce, particularly when things don't seem to work no matter how hard we try. It can be tempting to try to turn those emotions off by withdrawing. But as difficult as it can be at times to handle feelings, they are a vital part of us. They allow us to be fully aware, caring, intimate people. They connect us to others. It's important for us to accept our emotions even as we work to improve how we handle them.

A father's unhealthy emotional response to divorce or separation can be unfortunate for children. It can separate father from child. Many dads recognize this happening after a while. As time passes and their pain decreases they find themselves much better able to cope, and they become actively involved with their children in healthy ways.

If you recognize yourself in any of these common reactions—take heart! You are not alone, and things do get better. Keep in mind that the pain of separation affects not only you but your children's mother and your children as well. As you are struggling with your own pain, your actions make a difference in the lives of your kids.

We relate best to our live-away children when we concentrate on our own self-growth, and, at the same time, put our children's needs ahead of our own. These efforts are mutually reinforcing. As we concentrate on ourselves, we overcome some of our hurt and anger and are then more able to put our children first. When we put our children first, we provide them with direct help in the situations at hand, get closer to them emotionally, and take our minds off our own problems. Helping our children causes us to feel better about ourselves, and, as a result, our ability to meet our children's needs (and our own) improves even more. Improvements build on improvements, and things get better and better.

The Pain of Separation from Our Children Can Seem Overwhelming

When my daughters were younger, there were numerous times that my pain and loneliness were so strong that I felt like dropping out of parenting. The roadblocks to a close relationship with my kids seemed overwhelming. We usually had a very good time together, but we lived one hundred and ten miles apart, and the two-hour drive between their mother's home and mine was long for them and me.

They lived most of the time with their mother in a five-bedroom house with a big yard just blocks from their schools. I rented a one-bedroom apartment with virtually no yard. My daughters were not with me frequently enough to develop friends where I lived, so when they were with me it was just the three of us. At their mother's home they lived with their mother, their step-father, older stepsisters, and a new sister from their mother's second marriage.

When our daughters were with me I did what I could to make my home their home. During our two weeks together in the summers I got them into tumbling classes and other activities when I could find them. We spent time with my relatives. I made arrangements for them to play with children of my friends when possible.

I put off time for dating, seeing other friends, or working extra hours for when they were with their mother. I acknowledged their birthdays and other holidays with small presents, cards, or phone calls. I didn't spend much money on gifts, but I kept my daughters a presence in my life by my contact with them.

During difficult times, I often wondered how I could handle the hostility and pain of the divorce and the separation from my daughters. But *that I would handle it* was not a question. I might fantasize about dropping out at times, but I knew that I would never really give up my relationship with them. I wanted my kids in my life, and I knew they needed my support, my encouragement, my ideas, and my ability to listen and guide them. They needed my nurturing masculine energy and wisdom.

They needed my role-modeling of what a man is like. How I treat a clerk or waitress. How I talk about my job. How I relate to other men, women, and children. That I work hard and pay my bills on time. That I am physically strong but not dangerous. That I am competitive and like to be competitive and that it's okay to be competitive. That I enjoy roughhousing and being energetic at times but that I can also be gentle. That I like to get silly and I like to get serious. That I believe in the importance of success but that success is more than making lots of money.

They needed to know that I would be there for them forever. No matter what. They were little girls when I left their home. They were not able to know my importance in their lives. Knowing that is my responsibility. Their mother could not see my importance. She was blinded by her own pain and anger. It was my responsibility to stay involved.

Handling our emotions

Clearly, we don't want our emotional pain to get in the way of healthy fathering, but emotions do affect actions. Our behaviors are symptoms of the emotions inside, outward expressions of the way we feel. We can work on our behaviors without looking at our emotions, but that will limit our ability to succeed at our goals because we treat the symptoms (our behavior) without treating the cause (our emotions).

The extreme emotional pain of ending a relationship can be tremendous. It affects how we view almost everything that goes on in our lives. It is difficult to see things clearly when our vision is clouded by anger, loneliness, fear, sadness, or other emotions. When caught in this misery, many of us see the world through gray-colored glasses.

The magnitude of the distress caused by the ending of a relationship was really driven home to me when I worked as a psychotherapist in the inpatient psychiatric unit of a large hospital. The most common diagnosis for patients admitted to our unit was major depression. Many people were depressed for quite some time before entering our unit, but almost all admissions were triggered by some specific traumatic event in their lives. The most common of those events—by far—was the ending of a relationship with a spouse or lover. Seeing this again and again helped me understand the power that breakups have over people.

It's important that we be aware of our emotions as we deal with separation. Emotional awareness means conscious and accurate knowledge of our feelings. Without awareness, some people wallow in their pain or wear it like a badge. Others rage on endlessly and blame everyone else for their problems. Some pretend—to themselves and others—that it's not so bad. I hear them say they just want to "get this behind me." They tell me, "It's all in the past. Why get upset about it now? I can't do anything about what happened, so let's just forget it and go on."

But forgetting is not the same as healing. Trying to forget our pain just pushes it down. It does not allow us to deal with it. Healing means acknowledging, accepting, and expressing our pain as we allow time to pass.

In a divorce or other breakup there is plenty of hurt, guilt, and loss to go around—loss of a partner, normal contact with children, money, home, companionship, extended family, personal possessions, pets, self-esteem, future plans, trust, and friends.

I mention these losses not to make you feel worse but because you must acknowledge and grieve them to get past them. That might mean crying in sadness or ranting in anger—either by yourself or with people who support and understand you—but as you express these emotions they are released from you and you can get past them.

If you ignore or bottle up your hurt, it not only lasts much longer, it also boils, festers, and comes out in destructive ways—ways that may not seem connected to the loss at all. You yell at your children, kick the cat, quit a job, drink too much, withdraw from people, lose your temper, get into fights, or develop stomach problems and headaches.

The human mind and heart can only handle so much. If pain is not expressed in healthy ways, it will be expressed in others. Deep healing comes after you have more fully experienced your emotional losses. You can't just will yourself from pain to health. You must work through it.

Childhood affects the way we handle our adult emotions

Our emotional reactions to life depend on many things, but possibly the most powerful single influence is the way we were raised. Of course today's events and circumstances affect us also. Things such as physical health, our living situation, finances, employment, and support from others are important influences. However, our ability to trust others, the ways we handle our emotions, self-confidence, communications skills, self-understanding, and value systems have a strong influence over how we handle life today, and many of these traits were formed when we were children. We can change these traits consciously as adults, but it takes more effort.

Looking at childhood as a source of today's difficulties with emotions when we are twenty-five, forty-five, or sixty-five years old may not seem logical. It doesn't seem possible that, for example, our anger at our son's mother when we go to pick him up and, for the fourth time in a row, she doesn't have his things packed is really because we had a bad childhood! But in many very real ways it is. There is a powerful connection between the past and the present. Our parents did not sit us down and give us lessons on how to lose our temper, but they taught us how in their own actions every day.

This is not to say it's our parents' fault we have the problems we do. Our parents could have raised us better, but they also could have raised us worse, and *as adults, we are responsible for our actions today.* Making the connections between childhood and adulthood is simply a way to learn more about why we are the way we are. If we try to make changes without this understanding, it is more difficult.

Childhood experience affects our emotions as adults in three primary ways. It affects the intensity of our emotions, the variety of our emotions, and how we deal with that intensity and variety. Some homes allow strong emotional expression—high intensity. Some are subdued—low intensity. Some families encourage children to fully express whatever they are feeling without getting out of control; they allow the expression of a variety of emotions. Many more families limit expression. Unsure how to handle great anger, fear, sadness, or joy from children, parents put a stop to those emotions as soon as family members begin to express them.

Parents also unconsciously taught us how to express that variety and intensity of emotions. We learned by watching them. If we grew up in a loving, patient, calm, consistent home, we are likely to exhibit those characteristics as adults. If there was physical, verbal, sexual, or emotional abuse, negativity, parental absence, arguing, alcoholism, or other unhealthy parenting going on when we were growing up, we are more likely to handle our emotions less effectively as adults.

These childhood effects on adult emotions are very powerful, although they may also be very subtle. It's often difficult to see the connection between childhood and adulthood, but it's there. For the most part, anger is not inherited. It is learned. For the most part, fear or sadness is not genetic. It is a result of the million little ways that our childhood caregivers handled their lives—and ours.

I'm glad that it works this way, that our personalities and behaviors are not completely genetically determined. Genetics limit our potential. I'll never be six foot four no matter what I do or how hard I try. That's genetically determined. I'll never have the good looks of a movie star, even with plastic surgery. (Those guys are doctors, not magicians.) I can, however, learn to handle my anger better, communicate more effectively, and relate to my children more lovingly than my father did. These things are not genetic. They are within my control.

Four Stages of Emotional Growth

I've seen many men change how they handle their emotions, and the process usually involves four stages. These four steps seem to happen naturally, but your awareness of them may help you get through them more quickly and with less difficulty.

1. Acknowledge your pain

A lot of men were raised to hide their feelings. To many of us, it is not considered masculine to cry in front of others, show fear, or otherwise "lose control" of emotions. But because self-growth calls for emotional expression, the first step I often see men take as they are working on self-change is to allow themselves to experience their emotions a little bit more. They try not to block them from coming. When they are sad, for example, they say to themselves, "Yeah, I'm pretty gloomy right now." When they are mad they say, "Damn, I am so pissed off about this." They don't instantly get busy with other things or minimize their feelings—they acknowledge them.

2. Accept responsibility for your actions and commit to change

The second stage is when men accept responsibility for their actions and make a commitment to change. To do this they have to stop blaming others and blaming circumstances and work on their own change.

The acceptance of responsibility may come before, during, or after a commitment to change, but both must be present to move to the next stage. We commit to change by frequent reminders to ourselves that we want things to be better for our children and ourselves, and we accept responsibility by recognizing that we have the power to make things better.

3. Stop negative behaviors

After men acknowledge their pain and begin to take responsibility for their actions, the next step is often a conscious effort to stop their destructive behaviors. They try not to yell, swear, be negative, or hit. This is a very important step. Observable changes are made in this stage. Others often notice. As these men change, more positive things happen in their lives, and they develop more confidence in their ability to change. Some guys begin to feel good about themselves for the first time since the breakup.

4. Replace negative thoughts and behaviors with positive thoughts and behaviors

The fourth stage is one in which we *do positive things rather than stop doing negative things*. It involves a fundamental but gradual change in thoughts, feelings, and actions.

We replace our negative, angry actions with positive and supportive ones. We don't just stop hitting the dog, we pet it. We don't just stop complaining about people, we find good things to say about them. We don't just stop fighting, we start making peace. With continued work, improvements build on improvements, new insights develop, and positive things happen more and more often.

There is no great trick to moving through these stages. We succeed by doing. As the doing continues with conscious effort, we slowly learn more about ourselves and come to understand why we do what we do. Then we are even more able to make healthy decisions.

Because this process of growth is often unclear, it helps tremendously to have a good mentor on this journey. Seek out other positive people who support your efforts to change. Look for people who are respected and liked by others. Do as much of this as you can with men. As mentors, other men are the best teachers of how to become a strong and loving dad.

The next two chapters deal more specifically with two emotions that affect so many live-away dads and their children—anger and depression.

CHAPTER 2

Handling Anger

"A man should study ever to stay cool. He makes his inferiors his superiors by heat." —RALPH WALDO EMERSON

"Anyone can become angry—that is easy, but to be angry with the right person, to the right degree, at the right time, for the right purpose, and in the right way—this is not easy." —ARISTOTLE

In the months and years after your breakup, you may feel like you've gotten on with your life but are still experiencing a lot of anger. That anger can affect kids in several ways.

Children are very much like sponges, soaking up whatever they are immersed in. If their surroundings are safe, nurturing, and positive they will become confident, caring, well-adjusted adults. If they live in an inconsistent, negative environment, they will tend to be more fearful, angry, and argumentative.

In this chapter we will look at how anger affects kids and what you can do to more effectively channel the anger that you might have. As you read these pages, think of yourself, but also think of your own parents or other parent-figures who had a great influence on your life. And remember, looking at the anger of those who raised you is not judging or blaming them. It is simply a step toward understanding what life was like for you.

How patient, calm, and understanding were the people that raised you? What was their anger like? What did other people think of their frustration level? How often did they get mad, and what were they like when angry? What did you do when they were angry? How did you feel? Are there ways that you think their anger affected you as a child and now as an adult? Do you see similarities between how they were and how you are? Are there certain things they did that you have vowed you would never do?

Recognizing Anger

It's often very difficult for us to clearly identify our anger, because the majority of us were not raised to recognize or express it well. When our anger gets us into difficulties as adults, we try even harder to put it aside. When we try to put it aside we don't handle it well, and it comes out as verbal anger, physical anger, or both. Let's look at those two types of anger.

Verbal anger

Verbal anger is the most common type and includes behaviors such as swearing, name-calling, yelling, lecturing, complaining, negative statements, sarcasm, and the cold shoulder. Notice that some of these expressions of anger are what you say, some are how you say it, and one (the cold shoulder) is what you don't say.

It's easy to understand that yelling, swearing, and name-calling are expressions of strong frustration or anger, but it's harder to see the cold shoulder as anger. People giving the cold shoulder usually say they are just upset or frustrated. Those feelings are valid, but they are often stronger than people will acknowledge. There is definitely anger behind those icy cold shoulders.

Sarcasm is another form of anger that people have difficulty recognizing, even though it too is a clear indicator of anger. In fact, sarcasm is always hidden anger. Please pay more attention to any sarcastic statements you make. Is there any anger behind them at all? About anything? Even a little bit? When you hear sarcasm from others do you ever sense that they are angry? If so, recognize that your sarcasm carries hidden anger too.

Because the majority of us were not raised to express anger in a direct and healthy way, we express it as a joke, as little sarcastic comments. If anyone challenges us, we can say we were just kidding.

Comedians are some of the most intelligent—and angry— people I know. I greatly admire their ability to get to the truth of life with their humor, but I think for many of them it was the way they got by as kids. When they saw the injustice or craziness of their homes when they were little, they weren't allowed to express it directly, so they learned to cope with it by using humor. They had a knack for it, and it stuck with them.

The other night I heard a comic at a comedy club in town. He was talking about his parents. Part of his monologue went like this: "Yeah, my old man was a stitch. He hated summer, he hated vacations, and he hated driving—so naturally we went on a lot of driving vacations in the summer. Ha ha. And the three of us kids would get to arguing in the backseat. After a while he'd say something like 'If I have to turn around in this seat . . .' or 'If you make me tell you to shut up one more time, I'm going to . . .' Next thing I knew he'd flick his hand back and hit all three of us in the head with one perfect swing. Whack! Whack! Whack! Only guy I knew who could drive a car at sixty-five miles an hour in the dead of night, in the middle of a thunderstorm, arguing with his wife, and get us all with such pinpoint accuracy. Whack! Whack! Whack! Why, he'd get so mad he'd stop the car and hit other people's kids."

This comic was funny, but I'd bet a hundred dollars that something very similar to that happened to him as a child. And it wasn't very funny then. Most of us aren't professional comedians, but we can be pretty good at making anger sound like a joke if we aren't sure how to express it directly.

Physical anger

Physical anger includes any type of physical force when angry, such as hitting, grabbing, shaking, pushing, or pulling hair. Other forms of physical anger include breaking objects, slamming doors, and throwing things. If you break a glass because you are careless or in a hurry that's one thing. If you break a glass because you are pissed off and backhand it off the table, that's anger. Throwing a ball while playing catch with your child is a game; throwing the ball too hard, or at the ground in disgust, is anger.

Excessive Anger Affects Children

It's important to strike a balance in your anger. Some people are so quick to minimize their anger, or blame others for it, that they give up all responsibility for changing it. Their reluctance to take responsibility for being mad causes things to get worse and worse. Others (or the same people at different times) blame themselves too much for their anger problems. As a result, they become so bitterly critical of themselves that they are unable to change. You could say that their anger at their anger immobilizes them. When you get mad, it helps to look at yourself honestly without blame or denial.

There are several ways that excessive anger affects children, and one of the biggest ways is that it scares them. When strong anger is expressed around kids, they don't know what's going to happen next. They lose crucial self-confidence. It's just plain scary for kids, whether they are toddlers, preschoolers, preteens, or teenagers.

It isn't healthy for children to be afraid of their parents. There is already too much violence and aggression in the lives of many children today. Our job as parents is to help them deal effectively with that outside aggression and provide them with at least one place where they can feel totally safe.

Excessive anger can make kids depressed. Powerless to do much of anything about angry parents, they are left with no healthy way to control their environment. After a while they give up trying to change things. They withdraw. If that goes on long enough, some children eventually become depressed.

Children may show their depression through difficulty sleeping, overeating or undereating (sometimes both), a lack of interest in doing things they used to enjoy, excessive crying, anger, or aggression. They may avoid their friends, seem to care very little if they get into trouble, or perform poorly in school. They may have thoughts of hurting themselves or others, and, in extreme cases, they may attempt to harm themselves. If your children ever talk about hurting themselves it may be a warning sign of serious depression, and they should be taken to a counselor to look at the matter in more depth.

I recently worked with a divorced dad, Mike, and his eleven-year-old son, Leroy. Mike brought his son to counseling because he cried frequently, often five to ten times a week, and Mike didn't know what to do. Mike was a pleasant and outgoing dad who was very attentive and caring with his son. Leroy was a shy young man with a big smile and pleasant personality.

In our first session Mike acknowledged that he was sometimes too angry around Leroy, and when he was, it was usually about Leroy's mother. Almost every conversation Mike had with her ended with one of them storming off or slamming the phone down. Leroy loved both his parents, and the constant arguing was getting to him.

In our second session, which involved Mike, Leroy, and Mike's new wife, Leroy cried three times. Each time it was when his dad talked about not getting along with Leroy's mom. During the session I asked Leroy directly what made him sad. He sat there for a full two minutes without answering. I could see the agony on his face. Slowly, his eyes reddened. Tears rolled silently down his face and he whispered, "When mom and dad fight."

Near the end of that session Mike asked me what I thought made his son cry. In light of Leroy's words, I was surprised to hear the question. I pointed out to him what Leroy had just said, but he still didn't see it. As much as he cared about his son, his anger was blinding him.

Over the next several weeks Mike began to see how his anger affected Leroy. With that motivation, he began looking more closely at his arguing with Leroy's mother, and it decreased. In less than three months, Leroy's crying was almost completely gone.

Another effect of excessive anger around children is that it causes them to become angry themselves. If your actions show them that anger means yelling, getting even, refusing to talk, holding a grudge, or pretending not to care, they will tend to come up with unhealthy ways of expressing their anger.

Some dads feel that the demands upon them as adults are so great that it's okay for them to lose their temper once in a while— yet they react in anger when their children get mad. They don't seem to realize that their children's frustrations are just as big to them as adult problems are to grown-ups. These dads might benefit from being more patient with their children's anger and more careful with their own.

Anger also affects children if we try to ease our guilty consciences for losing our tempers by buying them clothes and presents or giving them excessive freedoms. If warring parents throw enough material objects their way, kids may even be fooled into believing that those things can make them happy.

What your children really want, of course (whether they know it themselves or not), is emotional intimacy with their parents. Material possessions can be worn out, lost, broken, or stolen. Emotional closeness can only improve your parent-child bond. Your children need your presence—not your presents.

Excessive anger robs children of their self-confidence, their belief in themselves and their abilities. Nurturing self-confidence in children is a little like building a table. That table begins as rough wood ready to be crafted. As we design it, work with it, shape it, screw it, and glue it together, we form it into a beautiful piece of furniture. When completed it will be strong and sturdy for many many years, but while it's still being put together it is delicate and easily damaged. A child's self-esteem is equally fragile.

Anger is also a factor in the all-too-common experience of children becoming aggressive, argumentative, or withdrawn when going from one parent's home to the other. Parents usually blame each other for this problem, but it's often quite difficult for outsiders to know which parent is the real culprit. Is it the frustrated father who has been short-tempered with his kids and complained to them about their mother, or is it the mad mom who interrogates the children upon their return to her house and reacts with anger to any nice things they say about their dad?

Children in the middle don't want parents to argue about who is to blame. They just want the anger to stop.

Handling Anger Successfully

We've looked at the problem, now let's look at solutions. There are some excellent methods for dealing with anger. A very helpful technique you can use starting today is the Quadruple-A method of anger management. If you want to work harder on your anger, get involved in individual counseling, support groups, therapy groups, or other types of help from others. They can be extremely effective. Either way, the Quadruple-A method can help. The four A's stand for:

1. Acknowledge—*Acknowledge* that you are angry
2. Assess—*Assess* your anger differently
3. Act—*Act* differently with your anger
4. Allow—*Allow* time to pass

1. *Acknowledge* that you are angry

Acknowledging your anger is the first step in conquering it. I see a lot of men minimize their anger by saying they are "a bit upset" or "concerned" when it is clear from the circumstance and their body language that they are fuming inside. But many of us don't think of ourselves as angry until we blow up.

Words like "frustrated," "upset," and "agitated," are actually just different types of anger. So it's often best simply to say you are angry. Acknowledge the anger directly so you can deal with it effectively. Then you can head it off before it gets out of hand. Recognize and acknowledge it as early as possible—while it is still small and manageable.

A good way to catch anger early is to acknowledge your very first thought about it. Many times we find ourselves thinking angry thoughts but ignore them in hopes they'll go away. But they don't. They often build until we blow up, unless we deal with them constructively.

Even before your first thoughts of anger, you may notice physical symptoms such as sweaty hands, a clenched jaw, red face, tight shoulders, or knots in the stomach, which are the results of adrenaline being pumped into the body. Learning to recognize these early warning signs of anger allows us to deal with our anger before it overwhelms us.

Actually, you can detect your anger even before the first thoughts and physical signs by acknowledging potentially explosive situations before they occur, situations such as picking your children up for your time with them or making a phone call to their mother. Before you enter those situations, acknowledge that you often get angry in them. Then say something to yourself such as, "I can feel myself getting angry at her," or "I can feel my jaw tightening and my hands opening and closing. This tells me I am starting to get ticked off." Doing these things allows you to channel your anger effectively, rather than having it sneak up on you.

Don't fear your anger or try to ignore it. Many people believe that thinking about their anger makes it worse. But the exact opposite is true. It's *not* thinking about it that allows anger to build up until it erupts. The Quadruple-A method, beginning with acknowledgment, gives you a way to get rid of that anger. Start by acknowledging how you really feel.

2. *Assess* your anger differently

Assess your anger differently to take away its destructive power. Many of us think of our anger as bad, but it's not. It's what we do with it that can be harmful. Anger is a powerful emotion, but one that responds to our beliefs about it. If we evaluate our anger as bad, scary, and harmful, it will become that. If we see our anger as empowering and useful, it becomes that.

Assessing anger differently requires self-talk (a conversation with yourself in your own head). Talk to yourself in a way that's open to the possibility of your anger being helpful. Self-talk yourself into assessing your anger differently. Try this: "I am really mad right now, but I can handle this and stay calm." Or, "My anger is not bad, it's what I do with it that counts, and I am going to handle it well."

Remind yourself of the times you've handled your anger constructively. Think about how this moment of anger will pass as time goes on. Feel good about saying to yourself that you have every right in the world to be as mad as hell, but that you also have the power to channel your anger constructively.

Dick and Marie

I met Dick and Marie when they came to me for marital counseling. Dick, a caring father with three sons, was a large man with a loud voice. He was often angry though, and when he argued with his wife, Marie, she would quickly cry. A lot of their counseling focused on anger work with Dick and assertiveness with Marie.

One day Dick told me that he and Marie had just gotten into one of the biggest fights they'd had in months. It started after the kitchen stove caught on fire while Marie was cooking lunch. It ended with a lot of yelling by Dick and crying by Marie. He was in the living room when the fire started. Marie screamed, and Dick scrambled into the kitchen to find flames shooting three feet above the stove. He immediately grabbed the fire extinguisher and put the fire out.

Dick spent a lot of time in session explaining why he had lost his temper with Marie. He related that he had been telling her for weeks to clean the grease off the stove specifically because he was concerned about the possibility of a fire. He feared that a fire could burn their house down. Someone could have been burned to death. If ever there was a dangerous situation this was it! If ever he had a right to be mad this was it! Right?

As I listened to Dick I found myself thinking he was more excited than angry. It soon became clear that he enjoyed telling this story. It had been an exciting adventure for him, and he had been the hero in it.

I said to him, "What were you so mad at her about?" In response, Dick repeated his list of reasons why the fire was such a terrible thing. "But," I replied, "the house didn't burn down. Nobody was hurt. Nothing was extensively damaged, and, besides, you too could have cleaned the grease off the stove if you were so worried about fires. Why do you lose your temper over something you had the power to prevent in the first place? Maybe your anger is more about the fact that she hadn't done what you told her to, and maybe if you assess your anger differently, you'd see that you were more excited than angry.

"It looks to me like you found the whole situation quite invigorating. I understand that this could have been a tragedy if someone had gotten hurt—but no one was. I can understand your fear of what might have happened, or joy and relief that no one was harmed, but all you expressed was anger. It almost seems as if you were looking for an excuse to lose your temper."

As we continued to discuss the fire and the fight, Dick began to see that he actually was more angry at Marie for not cleaning the stove than he thought and that he really had been as excited as he was angry. He began to see that his angry outburst had been more out of habit than anything else. He had confused his energetic response with anger. As Dick began to assess his anger differently, his mood improved considerably. He let go of lingering anger about the incident and replaced it with pride.

Like Dick, you can channel your anger more effectively when you assess it differently. Realize that your anger isn't bad—it's what you do with it that can be harmful. Anger is neutral, and you can, over time, learn to channel it to your benefit.

3. *Act* differently with your anger

After you acknowledge your anger and assess it differently, the next step is to act in different ways. You'll get many ideas of what to do differently in the following pages. Don't worry about making these changes instantly or perfectly. Little changes will eventually add up to big ones. Or as a friend once said to me, "Have patience. In time the grass will turn to milk."

Once when I was married I had an argument with my wife in the presence of her older brother. I went for a long walk to cool off afterward and came back about two hours later. When I returned I avoided people and was clearly "still in a bad mood."

After about twenty minutes of this, my brother-in-law said to me, "Bill, it's great that you went for a walk to cool off, but you are supposed to be less angry when you come back." That really struck me. He was right. I had returned almost as mad as when I left. I spent most of the time on my walk focusing on what I thought my wife had done wrong, and I had looked very little at my own part in the argument or how I could handle my anger better. I burned off some energy in my walk, and that was good, but it would have been even better if I had also paid more attention to my actions and made a conscious effort to come back less angry.

When I talk about acting differently I mean taking actions that specifically address the problem at hand, not just keeping busy. Men are often good at staying busy in the garage, the basement, or at work—so busy that we avoid our feelings. Sometimes working in the basement or listening to the stereo is a great way to let off steam, but at some point, you need to think about the conflict that occurred and do something positive about it.

In the following paragraphs I mention several things you can do to handle your anger better, some of which may seem awkward at first. Try them anyway. When you find some that work even a little, continue practicing them. As you stick with it they will become easier and more automatic.

Expend physical energy

When we are angry (or scared or excited), adrenaline is released to all parts of our body through the bloodstream. Adrenaline is sort of like fuel for the body and needs to be used up. Physical exertion is one of the best ways to safely burn it off. Go for a walk or run. Work out at the gym. Do push-ups until you are exhausted. Play tennis. Ride a bike. Go for a swim.

Talk with others about what's bothering you

At your job you may have to talk with coworkers to complete a task effectively. There are times in our personal lives when talking with others helps as well. Discussing problems with people you trust helps you come up with new ideas for handling those situations—a different way of looking at things when you get stuck in old patterns of thought. It also gives you a chance to get things off your chest. Just talking out loud releases pent-up emotions and makes you feel better. Talking about what happened—whether it was a fight with your children's mom or the disappointment of not seeing your kids—can have a freeing effect.

Many men were not raised to express feelings. We were taught to be tough and strong and independent, to handle problems on our own. But things are different now than they were forty, fifteen, or even five years ago. There are large numbers of men today who express their emotions more easily and are open to talking with you about what's going on.

You can discuss your situation with men or women, and both have a lot to offer. I used to talk primarily to women, but as I've gotten older it's become easier for me to talk with men. I like the direct way guys communicate, and I feel understood by them because we often have more things in common.

If you want to talk to men who'll listen, look for guys with a positive attitude about life. If you don't have anybody like that in your life right now, go out of your way to find and talk to guys in your family, at work, in church, or on your baseball team—men who are looked up to by others.

I'm currently working with a truck driver in counseling who is struggling with his marriage. The person he talks to is a positive, goal-oriented friend he's had for years. Another man I see in therapy works in construction. His older brothers are the people he talks to. They give him tremendous support and encouragement, which has been vital to his progress thus far.

I see another client, Pete, who works in a factory. He was devastated by his girlfriend's decision to break up with him. They have a son together, and at first Pete thought he couldn't live without them. He was depressed and angry for quite a while.

But Pete improved greatly after finding two men at work whom he could talk to when things got rough. Both of these guys were divorced but had never talked about it with Pete until he started telling them about his situation. Now Pete doesn't feel so alone. He vents his frustrations with these guys once in a while and gets solutions to problems he couldn't figure out on his own.

For more ideas and solutions that will help you act differently, go to chapter 13, "Support and Counseling Options Explained."

Express yourself creatively

Find a way to let your inner frustration out. Learn an instrument, carve wood, sketch, dance, act, sing, take up photography, rebuild a car engine, or express yourself in some other way. Do something new and positive that you've never done before. Keep a journal or write a mystery novel. Use paints to express your painful feelings or to escape them for a while. Don't worry about being good at your new activity. Just find something that's positive and fun.

Help someone else

Sometimes we get so focused on our own problems that we can't get our minds off them. A good antidote for that is to help someone else. Do some volunteer work at your church, community center, nursing home, hospital, day-care center, or school. Give someone a ride. Help your neighbor rake the lawn. Teach a child to ride a bike. Repair a broken screen door for a friend.

4. *Allow* time to pass

Once you've acknowledged your anger, assessed it differently, and acted differently, the final step is to simply allow time to apply its healing power. I don't know if this is the hardest part or the easiest. It's hard because time sometimes goes so slowly, but it's easy because time passes whether we do anything about it or not.

You'll heal sooner if you work on your own self-expression and self-growth as time passes, but even under the best of circumstances, some time must go by for you to recover. You can heal a broken leg in the quickest possible time by taking proper care of it. You can also further damage it by walking on it prematurely. But no matter how well you take care of it, there is a minimum time required for healing. Emotional wounds heal the same way.

CHAPTER 3

Am I Depressed?

"If we admit our depression openly and freely, those around us get from it an experience of freedom rather than the depression itself."
—DR. ROLLO MAY

I n the previous chapter I stressed that anger isn't bad, it's what we *do* with it that can be harmful. I think of depression differently. Depression is not bad, it's *what it does to us* that can be harmful. Anger shows itself as energy bursting to get out. Depression is a lack of energy. In anger we do things to others or even ourselves. In depression things happen to us. Another interesting way I have heard people describe the difference between anger and depression is that being mad at others is anger, while being mad at ourselves is depression.

Anger and depression also have much in common. They can both be extremely strong emotions and are often helped with the same techniques. In this chapter we'll look at some of those techniques, help you determine whether or not you might be depressed, see how that excessive sadness affects you and your children, and learn ways to overcome depression.

It can be difficult to know if we are depressed. Being in only one brain and body all our lives we don't know how others experience their emotions. We may know we are not happy, but we may not know if it's "bad enough" to get help. Men, in particular, don't want to look like whiners or weaklings. We think we have to solve our problems ourselves, and because of that, we are more likely to be depressed and not seek help.

This reminds me of what was going through my mind when contemplating my own divorce. The last three years of my marriage were unhappy ones for me. I often asked myself, "How bad is it for other people before they get divorced? Is it normal to argue this much? If I leave now am I quitting before other people would? Is there still a chance to work it out?"

People dealing with extreme sadness ask similar questions. How bad is this problem? How depressed do other people get? Can I get better on my own? Would it help me to go to a counselor? Is it normal to feel this bad for this long?

It can be difficult to distinguish depression from sadness, but one difference is that the severity and duration of the bad feelings are stronger and longer in depression than in sadness. When I see individuals in therapy it is standard procedure for me to ask them a series of questions to assess their possible level of depression. The following ten questions form the core of that evaluation. They are the specific problems and behaviors people often go through when depressed.

Ten Question Depression Self-Test

These questions will help you assess whether or not you may be depressed. They refer to the time period since your separation or the last few weeks or months since you have been feeling down. Go through them and mark each question within the ten that you answer with a "yes."

1. How is your appetite?

Have you lost your appetite? Do you eat just because you should? At the other extreme, do you think you eat too much or too often?

Do you eat beyond the point of being full? Do you eat out of boredom? Have you had a noticeable weight loss or gain since the time your problems started?

2. How well do you sleep?

Does it often take you forty-five minutes or more to get to sleep? Do you wake up at night and have trouble getting back to sleep? Do you have great difficulty getting up in the morning? Do you stay up late so you will be exhausted enough to go to sleep? Do you sleep too much, like ten or twelve hours per day? Have you been sleeping a lot more or a lot less since your problems started?

3. How is your energy level?

Do you often feel exhausted? Do you have trouble finding the energy to make it through the day? Do you often feel too tired to get out of a chair? Do you have a lot less energy than you used to? At the other extreme, do you find that you often can't stop moving? Does it seem like you often have a nervous energy that won't quit?

4. Do you find little enjoyment in doing things?

Have you stopped hobbies you used to enjoy? Do things that used to get you excited no longer have that effect? Does it seem that you just don't get pleasure out of doing things anymore? Could someone give you a valuable gift and you wouldn't even care?

5. Do you seclude yourself from people?

Do you stay in your room, apartment, or house more then you used to? Do you avoid even your supportive friends or family? Have friends or family asked why you don't come around anymore? Do you make excuses to avoid people because the truth is you just don't feel like being around them?

6. Do you have problems with memory or concentration?

Have you been more forgetful about where you put things? Do you have difficulty recalling names and appointments that you remembered in the past? Do you have difficulty concentrating on things now? Is it hard to read a book? Are you frequently worrying or daydreaming? Do you mess up at work because you can't seem to pay attention?

7. Are you frequently angry or irritable?

Do others comment that you overreact? Does it seem that you can't control your temper? Do you fairly often say or do things you later regret? Are you frequently moody or angry? Does your anger get you in trouble with others? Do you find yourself snapping at people?

8. Do you say a lot of negative things in your head?

Have you noticed that you think about yourself in very negative or angry words? Do you have thoughts like, "I'm stupid," "It will never work," or "I can't believe anybody would want to be around me." Do you say things to yourself like, "He is driving me crazy," or "She is making my life hell." Do you sometimes think about yourself in ways that seem bitterly angry?

9. Have you thought about taking your own life or killing someone else?

When asking my clients if they have thought of harming themselves, I usually say something like this first: "Now don't worry. If you tell me that you've thought recently of taking your own life, I am not going to overreact. I know that thinking about suicide does not automatically mean you will do it, and I have no desire or ability to have you locked up even if you are suicidal. What I do want to do is talk with you about what you are thinking and feeling so we can learn together if you are depressed. That way you can decide what you want to do if there is any depression."

Thoughts of killing someone else are much the same as thoughts of taking your own life, in that having them doesn't necessarily mean you will act on them. They do indicate, however, that you are at a level of sadness that could be dangerous and, at the very least, is unnecessarily painful.

Answer these questions. Do you say things to yourself like, "I don't care if I wake up in the morning," "People would be better off if I weren't around," or "I'm going to get her for good if this doesn't stop." Have you thought of specific things you have available to harm yourself? Have you planned how you would harm yourself or someone else? Have you ever taken any steps toward actually taking your own life or someone else's life?

10. Have you ever attempted to kill yourself or someone else?

Have you ever tried to take your own life or someone else's life? Have you ever been hospitalized for an attempt on your own life? Has anyone else ever received medical treatment because you harmed them physically out of anger? Have you ever stopped just short of an attempt to harm yourself or someone else?

Scoring

If you answered "yes" two or more times within any of the first eight sections above, give yourself one point for each of the eight. Give yourself two points each if you answered "yes" twice or more in questions nine and ten. Zero is the minimum score for this test and indicates no depression. Twelve is the maximum score and indicates extremely serious depression. If you score four points or more, I encourage you to consider seeking professional help.

This is not a complete test for depression. It's only a guideline. If you have any reason to think you might be depressed, regardless of the results here, seek professional help to discuss your situation further.

You do not have to be clinically depressed (diagnosed by a professional as depressed) to get help—and don't worry that your problem isn't bad enough to go for an interview with a counselor. If you have thought seriously about seeking counseling assistance, you would probably benefit from going. If you are concerned about feeling unhappy and overwhelmed, seek assistance. Let the counselor help you sort it out. Chapter 13 of this book, "Support and Counseling Options Explained," gives you helpful information about mental health professionals and how they can help you.

How Depression Affects Kids

Depression has many of the same effects on children that anger does but causes them in different ways. Let's look at four ways that depression may affect kids. I hope this will give you a better idea of the sensitivities of children. Sometimes we are reluctant to get assistance for ourselves, but when we realize that doing so could help our kids, we are more likely to get it.

1. Parental depression scares children

When a parent is very depressed and doesn't seem in charge of his or her own life, children may fear for the parent's safety or fear that they themselves won't be taken care of.

2. Excessive depression in parents creates anger or depression in kids

Depressed parents may avoid their children or respond angrily to them. Under those circumstances children may act out their frustration on themselves in the form of depression or on others in the form of aggression.

3. Excessive depression weakens the parent-child bond

Depressed parents often don't interact freely with their kids and tend to respond negatively. Since mutual fun is a part of any healthy parent-child relationship, parents and kids lose an important part of what their relationship could be.

4. Depressed parents are more likely to make poor decisions about their kids

Many parental decisions may be affected by depression, including the most important decision of all—to stay involved in their children's lives. If you are thinking of backing out of your child's life, get counseling assistance or support so that you don't. You are extremely important to your children and you help them tremendously when you stay in their lives.

There were times when I was very depressed after my divorce. I even thought of giving up on my kids and not seeing them anymore. It seemed that no matter what I did, nothing got better.

But as hard as it was, I took care of myself the best I could. I even went on antidepressants for several months. I hung in there, doing my best each day, believing and hoping and working on myself so that I could feel better, and I'm happy to say that things did get better—much better. If I had stopped seeing my kids for long periods of time, or terminated my parental rights, my pain would not have decreased. It would have become lifelong.

Overcoming Depression

Sadness is a normal and healthy reaction to difficult life circumstances, but excessively deep or long sadness is not healthy for anyone. That's depression. Loss of your children or their mother is a life-altering event. One in which a strong emotional reaction is understandable. But it is not good for you to suffer with serious, ongoing depression.

You have a right to enjoy your life, and your children need a healthy dad. If your sadness is a problem, work on getting better, but be patient with yourself. You will make many mistakes as you work on healing. At those times it is important that you don't get down on yourself. Do the best you can, and don't beat yourself up for being imperfect.

James came to me for counseling after his live-in girlfriend of six years, Pam, kicked him out of their apartment. They had two children together, ages five and seven. When James came to me he was quite depressed. He couldn't stop thinking about his kids and their mom. He'd hardly eaten or slept in the two weeks he'd been out of the house. Having nowhere else to go, he had been sleeping on a couch in his two-person contractor's office.

He denied thinking about suicide but admitted that he often didn't care if he woke up in the morning. He had seen his children twice since he'd moved out, and it was painful both times. He missed them and their mother. On top of this, business was very slow and he had too much time on his hands, so he thought a lot.

James talked nonstop in our sessions about how lonely he was, how angry he was with his kids' mom, and how scared he was that he wouldn't see his kids much in the future. He really needed to vent his frustrations and fears, and fortunately, I was smart enough to shut up and let him. I hardly said a word in those sessions. He didn't want any advice or suggestions. He just needed to talk.

After several sessions, and having told some of the same stories over and over, James began to feel more in control. He started coming up with ideas on his own of what he could do. One of the biggest steps was getting himself an apartment where he could feel comfortable taking his kids. After he did that, he began seeing them more and got some of his old energy, control, and self-respect back. He realized that he could indeed make it on his own.

Whether your reactions to your children or their mother are affected by occasional sadness or significant depression, it is possible to make changes. To deal with your emotions more effectively, use the same Quadruple-A method you learned in the previous chapter on anger. Begin by *acknowledging* that you are sad or depressed. Second, *assess* that condition differently. Third, *act* differently to deal with that sadness or depression more successfully. Fourth, *allow* time to pass as patiently as you can while you work on making things better.

1. *Acknowledge* that you are sad

The first step in dealing with depression is to acknowledge it. Lots of us men were raised to think of sadness as weakness. Over the years we put those sad feelings aside so often that they became hard to recognize. Today we go through our lives feeling "just fine" and "doing okay," but deep down we are numb.

Another rub with avoiding sadness is that it has a way of boiling over in anger or acting itself out as alcoholism, loneliness, isolation, ulcers, headaches, conflicts at work, sleep problems, or other things worse than the sadness itself. Ironic as it may seem, it is only in acknowledging and feeling our sadness that we begin to move beyond it.

2. *Assess* your sadness differently

Read the following five statements. Which, if any, do you agree with?

1. I must not show my sadness to other people.
2. Depression is bad.
3. I am weak or bad if I get depressed.
4. I must get over my sad feelings as quickly as possible.
5. There is little I can do about my sadness.

I agree with none of them. Depression is not bad, and we are not weak for feeling it. How we handle that sadness and how much it interferes with our life is important, but the feeling isn't bad in and of itself. Many men incorrectly think they must overcome their down feelings quickly and not show them to others. Certainly we don't want to wallow in those feelings, but the other extreme of hiding them can be equally harmful.

One example of a client overcoming depression by assessing things differently is the separated dad named Pete that I wrote about earlier. He was originally referred to me on an emergency basis by a relative of his, Andrea, who was in counseling with me at the time. She called me at home one evening from Pete's house because he had threatened to shoot himself. There were several guns in the house, and Andrea was very afraid that Pete would follow through on his threats.

After a lengthy phone discussion with both of them, Pete calmed down. He agreed not to harm himself. He also agreed to come see me the next day. In our counseling session the next day Pete told me that he was so upset about losing his son's mother that he couldn't enjoy his time with his son. Pete continued to struggle with depression for quite a while, but, in his case, improvement began as he made two realizations. One was that his relationship with his former partner was not as ideal as he had built it up to be. The other was that he was not the sole cause of their separation. Seeing things differently and letting go of his guilt helped him get over the hump, and he began to feel better.

Depression feels quite terrible, but it can also be seen as a signal to make changes in your life (seeing it as a signal is one example of assessing it differently). Don't assume anything about your depression. Be open to interpreting it differently and believe in your ability to overcome it.

3. *Act* differently with your sadness

After acknowledging your sadness and assessing it differently, your next step is to act differently based on that new awareness. During the depression I went through after my divorce, I couldn't seem to get rid of my down feelings, but I suspected that doing something—anything—would help me feel better. I'd often say to myself, "Okay, just do something, Bill. Get off your lazy ass and clean the house, read a book, get some work done around here, or call the kids, but *do something!*"

The improvements made by "doing something" weren't always

apparent back then. I couldn't quite tell if doing things actually made me feel better. To make things worse, if I tried to get myself to do something and couldn't, I'd get mad at myself for that! Strange as it may seem, there were times when I was almost glad to be depressed. At least then I didn't have to worry about *becoming* depressed. As much as I hated it, there was safety in being in that hollow.

Looking back at it now, I recognize that doing things did help in the long run. I remember one of the things that was most helpful to me. Doing the dishes. It may sound dumb, but it worked for me. Doing dishes got me started. Then I could sometimes move to doing other things I wanted to do. If I got that far I was usually starting to feel better and at least got satisfaction about accomplishing something that day.

Doing something was one of the things that worked for me, and it might work for you. In the following paragraphs I make several suggestions of things to do. I've found that they are effective with anger too, so feel free to try them out for that as well. When you find ones that work even a little bit, keep doing them, and keep trying new things to see if you can find more weapons to use in your anti-sadness arsenal.

Get physical exercise

The mind and the body are closely connected. Physical exercise keeps the body strong and the mind sharp. Regular exercise leads to improved self-esteem, more stamina and strength, better use of free time, and even new friendships with other physically active people.

Do relaxation exercises

There are many relaxation exercises you can do to release tension and increase energy at the same time. There are many good books on relaxation techniques, and I encourage you to get one and use it. I can suggest one simple exercise here. It's called Three Deep Breaths. It can be used anywhere and only takes a couple minutes. Use it any time you are feeling sad, angry, or nervous.

For this exercise, simply stop whatever you are doing, stand or sit straight, shake your shoulders out a bit, rotate your head down and around in all four directions a couple times, then come to rest and take three deep, slow breaths (do a few more breaths if you want). Close your eyes if you like. Breathe in deeply, hold the air for one to three seconds, then let it out slowly or quickly, depending upon what feels best at the time.

When taking in the deep breaths, think of good clean air coming in and circulating to all parts of your body. Visualize it spreading all the way to your fingers, head, and toes. While exhaling, think of all the rotten, mucky, negative air being expelled. For a minute or two after this exercise, consciously move slowly, and don't talk out loud. Allow yourself to carry the calmness with you for a while.

Eat well

Food is fuel for the body, and if we supply our body with good foods in moderation, our physical and mental performance will be improved. The basics of proper eating are pretty common knowledge by now (although still hard to actually do) so I simply encourage you to do the best you can. No guilt trips here. Eat well when you can, but don't beat yourself up if you can't.

Get enough sleep

There are no two ways about it, the body and mind need rest to function properly. Many dads are constantly on the go, working long hours—and it shows. They are exhausted and cranky. Regardless of how busy you are, do your best to get enough sleep—if not for your own sake, then for the people around you.

Work in moderation

We need to work to support ourselves and our families, and child-support payments put even more work pressure on live-away dads. Work can also be a tremendous source of personal satisfaction and pride. Problems occur, however, when work becomes an obsession. Then, instead of building families, it destroys them.

Many men were raised to define themselves through their work. We became competitive about earnings and possessions. We even fooled ourselves into thinking those things could make us happy.

To assess if work might be a problem for you, answer "yes" or "no" to each of the following questions: Has anyone ever told you that you work too much? Has anyone close to you (child or adult) ever complained that you care more about work than them? Do you go to work, or stay there longer than necessary, to avoid problems at home? Do you think you would have little purpose in life if you couldn't work? Do you lose vacation time because you're too busy to take it? Do you sometimes think you might be a workaholic?

If you answer "yes" to two or more of these questions, look at the role that work plays in your life. It may be wearing you out and keeping you emotionally distant from your kids and others.

Avoid excessive use of alcohol or other drugs

Excessive use of drugs and alcohol is an attempt to escape problems. People often feel less inhibited when under the influence of alcohol, but because it is actually a depressant, it makes them more depressed in the long run. When you get high rather than deal with your feelings and their causes, problems mount up. Your depression and isolation increases, and more alcohol or other drugs must be consumed to "feel good" again. It becomes a vicious cycle.

Find strength through a higher power

Many people derive tremendous strength from a source outside themselves. They call on that power frequently and never feel alone because of their faith.

Take a risk

We increase self-confidence by trying new things, whether we succeed at them or not. By risking involvement in things we've never done before, we open ourselves up to new ideas and opportunities.

Several years ago a dad joined an anger management group I

conducted. His girlfriend had just left him, and he was a wreck. He was losing his temper with everyone and could hardly concentrate at work. Because that particular group was not designed for live-away dads, it was not an ideal group for him, and he only attended five meetings before quitting. In those five meetings, however, he visibly improved.

Why did he get better? In my opinion there were two primary reasons. The first was that he talked things out, and the second was that he had taken a risk. He had been afraid to join any group before this one. When he finally faced his fear, he showed himself that he could do things that he thought he couldn't.

Spend more time with people

We all need time to ourselves, but intentionally avoiding people because you are too down or ashamed to be with them isn't healthy. During my marriage, almost all of my socializing was done with my wife and other couples. After I moved out of the house, the couples we used to hang out with didn't know how to deal with us. I didn't fit in as the third person going out with a couple, and I had no close male friends to do things with.

A couple of weeks after I moved out of my house, I was invited to supper at the home of a coworker and her husband. They were nice people, but I had never spent time with them outside of work. I'm sure they invited me because they knew how lonely I was. I accepted their invitation out of social obligation.

I didn't think I'd feel comfortable spending an evening with them, and I turned out to be right. We had supper, I stayed another hour or so after it and went home. I was uncomfortable the entire evening but will always remember that night as a positive one because, at least for a while, I was with people who cared about me. I really appreciated their kindness, and it was important for me to be with people when it would have been easier for me to withdraw. For a couple of hours I was less lonely than I would have been by myself. I was doing something positive for myself.

If it seems that you have no one to be with, take the risk of seeking out friends, coworkers, or family members, and get together with them. Notice that I didn't suggest getting a new girl-friend. Jumping quickly into another relationship doesn't allow time for personal growth. Regardless of how different this new woman may be, you need time to learn more about yourself and overcome some of your emotional pain. Until you do that, you are at great risk of repeating your previous mistakes in your new relationship.

Change your self-talk

Self-talk is that little conversation we have in our head. Some people call it internal dialogue. Self-talk can be very complex: "How do I deal with being alone?" Or it can be simple: "I'm starved. What can I find to eat?" It can be negative: "I'm so stupid, there's no way I'll ever do it." Or it can be positive: "I know if I keep trying I'll find the solution to this problem."

Become more aware of your internal dialogue. Recognize how you talk to yourself. Use your self-talk to ask yourself, "What did I just say to myself?" Look for patterns in how you talk to yourself. Is your internal dialogue positive or negative? Is it loving and patient or angry and anxious? Is it critical or friendly?

If you notice that your self-talk is negative or blaming, consciously replace it with positive self-talk. Do this over and over until it comes more easily. Even in situations where negatives must be acknowledged, find something positive to say as well.

As I've looked at my own self-talk over the years, I've learned a lot about myself. I used to think of myself as an optimist. But as I listened more closely to my self-talk, I began to realize that I was more of a pessimist than I'd thought. As I continued to pay attention to my thoughts, I began to see that I was also a realist. Since then I've coined a word for what I probably really am, an "omnimist," a combination of optimist, pessimist, and realist. Paying more attention to my self-talk helped me know myself better, and, in the long run, that self-knowledge allows me to enjoy my life more.

Practice positive affirmations

Positive affirmations are brief statements you repeat to yourself several times a day. You can say them in self-talk or out loud. They may feel forced in the beginning, but if repeated enough they begin to come more naturally. When you use affirmations frequently enough, you sort of fool your mind into believing them.

To come up with a positive affirmation, think of something you want in your life, and state it in positive terms. The wording of affirmations is very important. Be sure that you say what you can do, not what you can't (a pretty good idea for any thoughts you have).

For example, say "I will remain calm," rather than "I will not lose my temper." Rather than say to yourself "I am not going to let my kids get on my nerves today," say something like "I am going to be relaxed with my kids today." See the difference? Positive affirmations state what you are aiming for in positive terms, not what you are avoiding.

Some people state positive affirmations ten or so times each morning and night, while others repeat them five to fifteen times at various points throughout the day. I'm not sure it matters so much when you do them as that you do them on some consistent basis. The following are affirmations you might use to change your thinking:

"I am more patient with my daughter."
"I feel better every day."
"I am beginning to make friends at work."
"Work is going well today."
"I stand up for myself in positive ways."

Use these affirmations and come up with your own. Make sure they are in positive terms and state what you want to be true. People sometimes make fun of positive affirmations. They joke about these "touchy-feely" ideas. Some of the jokes are pretty funny, but they make fun of techniques that have been around a lot longer than the jokes have. I urge you to give affirmations a try.

Make use of creative visualizations

Creative visualizations are pictures we form in our head of what we want. Some people call this picture "in the mind's eye." If, for example, you feel angry or discouraged on your way to pick up your kids for the weekend, visualize yourself driving down a beautiful sunny street smiling broadly as you energetically wave to everyone you see. Everyone notices you instantly and waves back enthusiastically.

Visualizations can be even more effective when combined with positive affirmations. Using them together, you not only visualize yourself driving down the street feeling fantastic, but you also say something to yourself like "I feel really great right now." Exaggerate your mental image. In this example, you might picture yourself twenty feet tall in your gigantic shiny car.

Here's another instance of how you can combine an affirmation with your visualization. Let's say again that you are going to pick up your kids from their mother's house. A helpful visualization might be to see yourself walking up to her house in a confident, calm, and controlled manner. Form a picture in your head of you keeping the exchange brief and courteous. Visualize things going beautifully, with the sun shining and you looking great. See your children and you smiling as you leave together for an enjoyable and productive day.

Accompany that image with an affirmation like this: "This will go great, and I will remain calm during the whole time I'm at her house." When you get to the house, you might change the affirmation to present tense and repeat it as: "Things are going great, and I am staying very calm." As you leave the house, repeat to yourself something like "I was calm the whole time, and I am heading off into a great day." This statement is a reward and reinforcement you can give yourself.

You can use visualizations and affirmations any time you approach an anxious situation or even right in the middle of one. Develop your own visualizations and affirmations for specific situations you encounter. If you have some that are particularly helpful, use them over and over.

Give yourself reminders
Leave yourself written notes in various places as reminders of your goal or how you want to conduct yourself. To deal with de-

pression they might be something like "I'm feeling good today," or "I'm assertive with people." These are statements much like positive affirmations, except they're written. You can leave them on your dashboard, in your wallet, on the bathroom mirror, in a drawer, or any other place that works for you.

4. *Allow* time to pass

As with anger, part of healing depression is allowing time to pass. Depression feels so bad we want it to go away right-now-forever, but because change is a process and not an event, it takes a little time. Be patient. Work on self-improvement, keep putting your children's needs first, and allow time to pass.

The purpose of Part I has been to learn how to take care of yourself—because you have the ability and the right to feel better, and because feeling better will help you be a more loving father to your children. There are many things you can't control in your life, but you can control your own actions and how you deal with your own emotions.

Many of us fathers were raised as children to be tough and independent, and our natural nurturing skills were not emphasized. When faced with the tremendous challenge of fathering from a distance, too many of us have walked out, just as some of our own fathers walked out on us—literally or emotionally. But your love and commitment to your children can change all that. You've started taking care of yourself here, and you will discover more about getting along with others, dealing with the courts, fathering, and getting support for yourself as you read on. You are extremely important to your children. Continue on in this journey.

PART II

Getting Along with Your Children's Mother and Others

Fathers face special challenges to their patience and strength after separation from their children. At times it may seem impossible to get along with your child's mom and others. But you can do so by being creative and flexible.

Getting along with others requires knowing when to push and when to let go. Many men were raised to fight for what they want, but sometimes, particularly in personal relationships, we achieve more by fighting less. We win by letting go of winning at all costs. That way we reach compromises that truly nurture us and our children.

An old oak tree is huge and strong, but there are even greater forces of nature around it, so the oak tree also bends under the fierce and powerful force of storms. Then it continues to grow as it nurtures and protects the young saplings beneath it. The majestic old oak tree lives long because it is strong—and flexible.

CHAPTER 4

Succeeding with Your Children's Mother and Her New Partner

"Everything that irritates us about others can lead us to an understanding of ourselves."   —CARL JUNG

Dealing with Your Children's Mother

Children need to know that their parents back each other up and support each other in their parenting. But how do you support your children's mother when you disagree with her? You do it by keeping disagreement civil, making compromises, not cutting her down, and focusing on your goal of putting your children first. It's amazing how powerful that goal can be when you understand its importance and commit yourself to it.

Some fathers drop out of parenting. It seems to them that they have an impossibly long time ahead of them before conflicts with their former partner will end, child support will be over, and their kids will be on their own. But I encourage you to stay involved for the long haul in spite of these difficulties. Your relationship with your kids goes far beyond their eighteenth or nineteenth birthdays, and putting them first is the best way you have of ensuring that they will want to be around you now and during the many more years that they are adults.

In this chapter we look at ways you can work constructively

with your former partner and others as you continue to work on yourself. You cannot change your children's mom. Your power lies in working on yourself and growing beyond dependence on her.

Some live-in moms are almost impossible to deal with. Some are very reasonable. Regardless of which you consider your children's mother to be, you can't control her—*but you can always control how you deal with her.*

There is a ceiling on the level of cooperation that can be reached between the two of you. That ceiling consists of the uppermost limits that both of you have in constructively dealing with life. No matter how you approach her, she'll never go beyond her uppermost limit. But her ceiling is a high one, as is yours, and you have a lot of influence over how close she gets to her uppermost limit. How close that is depends quite a bit on how well you deal with situations that come up. The better you are at expressing yourself, working cooperatively, and making healthy decisions, the more those behaviors will provide an atmosphere in which she can raise her skills.

I imagine some fathers think as they read this that I want them to keep peace by letting their children's moms have their way. That is not the case. I'm not suggesting that you give her whatever she wants every time you deal with her any more than I suggest that you fight with her constantly. My ideas are about doing things in that difficult to find but ultimately productive middle ground. That place where you know yourself and stand up for yourself, but you respect others while you do it. Not standing up for yourself is as damaging as bullying her, and both are less effective than finding that middle ground.

An example of middle ground

It's hard to stay calm yet assertive, especially if your children's mom doesn't, but that's the challenge that may be before you. One dad, Michael, sought the middle ground after his former wife, Lynn, remarried. One day he heard his son and daughter refer to their stepfather as "dad." The first chance Michael had to speak with Lynn alone, he let her know that was not acceptable to him.

When Michael's kids were young, Lynn had gone so far as ask his permission to have the kids adopted by her new husband. He was shocked. He couldn't believe she would even think he'd consider it. Michael was current on child support, spent time with his kids frequently, and was much more involved with their teachers and school than their mother. He saw her request as an indication of how little she knew about his connection to their children, and it reinforced his commitment to stay involved.

Michael told me he was prepared to fight Lynn in court to stop their children from calling their stepfather "dad." He had no idea what the judge would have done with something like this but was prepared to find out. He knew that there were lots of things he had no control over in the way his children were raised, but he was willing to do anything legally necessary to see that they clearly understood what his role was in their lives.

Fortunately Lynn agreed to this change and had Michael's kids call her new husband by his first name instead. I found it somewhat unusual for children to call a stepparent by their first name (a nickname or other invented name of some type is often a good alternative), but it was a good solution in this case. It's often difficult for separated parents to find that middle ground, but that's what Michael did. He stood up for himself but maintained his composure.

Stop Conversations from Becoming Destructive Arguments

Many live-away dads find they are unable to have conversations with their children's moms without arguments, in spite of repeated attempts to do so. One angry thought here leads to an angry word there, which is followed by an accusation about this resulting in blame about that. Pretty soon things are completely out of control. It becomes a struggle just to avoid a shouting match or physical fight.

A first step toward calm can be to let your former partner know you are trying to decrease conflict with her. Ask her if she would be willing to work with you on developing rules for your conversations. If she is, try to agree on what you will talk about early in each conversation, and end discussions when either parent goes off the subject. Set up a code word or phrase that either of you can announce to stop conversations from getting out of hand, a "time-out." Agree together what code word to use and what will happen when it is stated.

For example, you might mutually agree that the phrase "end conversation now" or "time-out" means that the person who says it can hang up the phone, end that conversation, or leave the area. Use of this code word must also include a commitment by the person who calls it to reconnect with the other parent in a certain time period (two hours or three days, for example). That way you can finish the conversation when you are both calmer, and things don't get put off forever.

If you can't both agree on rules of communication, there is still a lot you can do on your own.

First, think about the behaviors or topics that get the two of you arguing. Write down one or two things she does and one or two things you do that most often lead to arguments. These are your flash points.

Second, plan in advance what you will do when a flash point occurs. Let's say, for example, that a flash point for you is your former wife bringing up money when you need to discuss your daughter getting into trouble in school. You may decide that every time your child's mom brings up money you will tell her you aren't going to discuss it when the topic is school. Remind her that your goal is to avoid arguments. Offer to discuss money at a later date, and take a minute to decide upon that future time.

As part of your advance planning, think what your response will be if she doesn't drop the money issue. That might include telling her you will end the conversation if she doesn't stop. If you are talking with her in person, tell her you are ending the conversation and leave immediately. If you're on the phone, tell her you are going to hang up, and do so. Say these things without yelling, name-calling, or swearing. In one or two sentences, explain what you are doing, but don't get dragged into a fight, and don't try to convince her you are right. Those are seeds for another argument.

Here's an example of what you might say if your child's mom keeps getting off the subject: "Annie, I just called to talk about Rosalinda getting sent to the principal's office. Let's not talk about money now. If you want, I'll call you Saturday morning to discuss finances." If she continues to bring up money, you may say something like "I just called to talk about Rosalinda and school. I don't want to get into an argument. I've told you I'll call about the money Saturday. If you insist on bringing money up now, I will hang up."

If she continues to talk about money, say good-bye and get off the phone without further discussion. Remember that your purpose in doing this is not to hurt her; it is to end a conversation that would otherwise get out of hand.

After having discussions end this way a few times, she may begin to see that she must stay on the topic at hand if anything is going to be accomplished. This, of course, goes both ways. You may have to end conversations when you can't stay on track, and if she uses this method with you, fight your urge to get the last word in. The more the two of you respect the other's right to head off trouble, the better you'll communicate over time.

Of course, ending conversations is not always practical. There are times when, for example, you need to pick up your children or finalize plans to be with them, and ending the conversation without making those arrangements would deprive you of seeing them. In those cases, you might try the broken-record technique. Simply repeat the same sentence—like a broken record—each time she hits one of your flash points.

An example of the broken-record technique would be when you call your former partner to confirm what time you will pick up your son for the weekend, and she starts an argument about how the two of you will divide your CD collection—a flash point for you. Since you must make arrangements about the weekend, you need to find a way to keep the conversation productive.

Start with a calm and direct statement like "Annie, I don't want to discuss the CD collection now. I called to confirm when I will pick up Roger for the weekend. Let's decide about that and discuss the CDs later." If she goes back to the subject of dividing CDs, repeat your statement—do not get pulled into arguments, defend your position, or prove you are right. State again, "Annie, I don't want to discuss the CD collection now. I called to confirm when I will pick up Roger for the weekend. Let's decide about that and discuss the CDs later." Continue using identical sentences every time she gets on the subject of CDs in that conversation.

If you say you will discuss the division of CDs at a later date, you've got to follow through. If you don't, she will not trust you in the future. The broken-record technique is a method to avoid arguments—not a trick to avoid discussion.

In all meetings with your child's mother, use your brain. Don't let your anger control you. You have a right to be frustrated with her, but be smart. There is nothing to be gained by venting your anger at her. Find ways to work things out.

Ten Commandments of Communication

In the suggestions above I've presented some specific ways to deal with verbal conflicts that arise between parents. The Ten Commandments of Communication, on the other hand, provide guidance on ways to conduct yourself in almost any situation or interaction that comes up between you and your children's mother.

1. Know yourself

You will deal most effectively with your children's mom if you know yourself well. Stop once in a while to think about your needs and motives. Examine your thoughts, feelings, and actions. Don't just react to her—have a clear understanding of yourself and what is important to you.

Steve, a dad in his midforties, has never married but had a child with a woman, Karen, when he was twenty-two years old. After Karen became pregnant she stopped seeing him and made it clear that she wanted nothing to do with him as a partner or as a father to their son, Kevin.

Steve accepted this at the time, but when Kevin was sixteen years old Steve contacted Karen about seeing his son. At that point Karen agreed, and Steve, who now lived several hundred miles away, began to see Kevin. This relationship started out well for both of them, but as time passed they seemed to drift apart.

Steve was touchy, even secretive, about this relationship and would not listen to feedback from others. He didn't seem to know what he wanted for himself, his son, or Karen, and he and his son became more distant. In this case, Steve's not knowing what he wanted didn't cause conflict, but it prevented intimacy.

Know your own strengths and weaknesses and what type of relationship you want with your children—and their mother. With that understanding you make better decisions and are more self-directed. Ultimately, you end up getting more of what you want and so does your child.

2. Never follow, threaten, harass, or physically harm your former partner

This sounds obvious, but as many dads could tell you, it's often easier said than done. Being away from a lover or our children can be extremely painful, and at those times we are most likely to do things we wouldn't otherwise do.

Some men are greatly tempted to follow or harass their children's mother. Their loneliness and loss of control seems overwhelming, and it takes great effort on their part to avoid such behaviors. Do whatever you need to do to avoid threatening or harassing your children's mom, because actions such as those are unfair to her, distance you from your children—and have the potential to land you in jail.

If you are struggling not to harass her, it helps to remind

yourself of what can happen to you if you do hassle her. Let off steam by talking to friends or other live-away dads. Reread the chapter on anger. Do physical exercise until you are exhausted. Take up new hobbies or activities to fill your time. Develop other interests so you are not so preoccupied with her.

3. Keep conversations brief (but not too brief!)

Many men were raised to be strong, silent, and to focus on solutions. Unfortunately our emphasis on silence and solution can lead to problems with communication, saying too little or saying too much.

As boys, many of us were not encouraged to look at and express our emotions as much as girls were. Some of us came to think that talking is for girls and action is for boys. As adults, we sometimes feel inadequate in conversations with women and give up talking before we even start. We remain silent.

Too much focus on solutions has many drawbacks also. We may not recognize or accept when we have gotten all we can out of a situation. We push for solutions and damage communication.

Find that middle ground between talking too little and too much. Say what you need to say, but listen and compromise as well. Stand up for yourself in conversations with your children's mother, but also know when to quit. If you don't, all conversations with her become toxic and communication dies.

4. Stick to the point

When you talk to your children's mom on the phone, at the house, in court, or anywhere else, stick to the point. If you are both there to talk about your child's school performance, talk about that—not how she spends your child support. If you are there to talk about child support, talk about that—not her boyfriend. It's easy to get off the topic and argue about a million things, but doing so only poisons current discussions and makes future positive ones difficult.

Set aside a separate and specific time to work out conflicts. Some parents I know make a point of having conversations about the kids only after the children have gone to bed. Others separate conversations about the children (grades, sibling fights, baby-sitters, schedules) from conversations about adult concerns (money, property, relationships, grandparents). Stay on the subject.

5. Stay in the present

Few things destroy a discussion about current problems more quickly than bringing up the past. Why does the past so often come up between separated parents? Because it's not yet resolved. We haven't moved beyond it.

Some of us bring up the past because we haven't gotten on with making a good life for ourselves now. We've become too dependent on our children's mother to make our life work out today.

Others of us keep bringing up past mistakes because we want to hear our children's mom say, just once, "Yes. I was wrong. It was my fault. It won't happen again." But we rarely (never?) get that hoped-for response, and, even if we do, it won't be enough, because that's not the real issue. The real issue is our own anger, grief, and lack of control. Dealing with that can move us ahead. Bringing up the past won't.

A Vietnam veteran I once worked with in parenting-time mediation, Dave, was obsessed with the past. He and his wife, Kate, had been divorced for several years. Dave was constantly trying to get her back, but, at the same time, he constantly pushed her away by pointing out her past mistakes. Kate still wanted to be with Dave, but whenever she tried to get close to him he'd bring up the past, and it ruined the present.

If you find yourself focusing on the past, concentrate on the present. Remind yourself to stay in the here and now. When you find yourself bringing up the past, as difficult as it is to do so, stop in midsentence and change the subject.

6. Develop and use a conversational style

Mistrust and anger between parents can make it unbelievably hard to talk calmly, but one way to prevent outbursts is to have an idea in your head of the type of conversation you want to have. You used to talk to your children's mom as a lover. What takes its place now? "Businesslike" may be a good fit, but because there are such strong emotions between the two of you, being businesslike may come off as distant and hurtful. "Enemy" might feel accurate at times but wouldn't get you very far either.

I suggest that you try to talk to your child's mom in a way that I would describe as "civil." Before conversations with her, picture yourself speaking in a civil manner to a salesperson, in a calm way to an acquaintance, or constructively with a boss you disagree with.

Take a minute right now to find a conversational style you are comfortable with. Try it out loud. Experiment over the next few weeks to come up with one that fits in the midpoint between attacking her and freezing her out. Find an approach that respects both of you. Keep that image and sound in your head as you speak with her, and bring yourself back to it when you find yourself talking otherwise.

7. Assert yourself

One of the most common mistakes men make in communicating with their children's mom (or women make in communicating with their children's father) is being too passive or too aggressive. They have trouble finding that assertive middle ground. The trick to being assertive is to say what you need to say—but not cram it down her throat. Keep in mind that she has as much right to disagree with you as you have to ask for what you want.

If you are upset about how she disciplines the kids—say so. If you believe the people she spends time with are a bad influence on the kids—say so. If you want to be with the children more—say so. But don't harp on these points. Tell her what you want, but don't demand to get it. Saying nothing to her is ineffective. Telling her what you want a few times is assertive. Saying it twenty or thirty times is obnoxious.

One way to assert yourself is through the courts. If you see a problem that you think is serious enough for you to involve the legal system, do so. Used wisely, courts are a good way of asserting your rights without personal attacks. The next section of this book, "Navigating the Court System," will help you in that.

8. Be honest about your actions

To promote openness and compromise between your children's mom and yourself, be truthful about your own actions. This means acknowledging and admitting your part in arguments and your mistakes. You need not tell every fault you have to anyone who'll listen, but if you want your children's mom to be honest about her mistakes, you have to be honest about yours.

Let her know if, for example, you think you were too hard on her in an argument or were late for an exchange of the children simply because you forgot. Don't make excuses. Explain what happened, and try not to do it defensively or with anger. Try to adopt the civil conversational style you are experimenting with from commandment number six. This will invite her to respond with equal calmness to your information rather than with anger at your anger.

It's difficult to be completely honest with your children's mother, particularly if she is not honest with you, but it has to start somewhere if you ever hope to communicate well with her. Hopefully your honesty will lead to more honesty on her part. It often does, but there are no guarantees it will, and that is not the purpose for your honesty anyway. Your honesty is about personal integrity. Regardless of what your children's mom does, you maintain your integrity as a man and serve as a positive role model for your children by acting with honesty in your life.

9. Work with your children's mother on parenting

Children need a united front from their parents, even when they live apart. If you don't support your children's mother in her parenting, the kids will become manipulative and rebellious. If she raises them differently than you would, talk with her about your concerns away from the children, and support her in front of them.

If you continually find yourself in strong disagreement with her parenting strategies, one of two things is probably happening. Either, in your pain and anger, you are overreacting to her, or she is making poor parenting choices. If you think you may be overreacting, work on your own emotional pain, and support her parenting. If you are convinced that she makes poor parenting decisions, do your best to determine how harmful they are.

If you believe that she is harming the children, and you've told her directly what you want her to change, you may be best off going to court to let the mediator or judge look at it. If you do so however, and the court makes no major changes in how she must parent, recognize that you are overreacting to her—or at least that the courts will not change things.

Regardless of what your children's mom does, cooperate with her as much as you can, and keep your kids out of the middle. It may be extremely difficult to change how you relate to your children's mom, but from what I've seen with other dads, it's less exhausting and more helpful than constantly fighting.

10. Don't attempt to be perfect

Your children's mom makes mistakes and so do you. Don't pretend to her, your kids, yourself, or anyone else, that you are perfect. Trying to be perfect puts too much pressure on you and comes off as phony. Work to improve things for your sake and the sake of the people close to you, but don't become obsessed with perfection. You aren't going to stay close to your kids if you are constantly critical and uptight.

Dealing with Your Children's Mother's New Partner

The relationship that men have with their former wives' new boyfriends or husbands can range from mutual respect and cooperation to profound hatred. Your emotional pain can be extreme if you have no one to be with yourself, he is the one she left you for, or, worst of all, he treats your children badly. Yet you are expected to interact with this person calmly. It is a monumental task. Sometimes a daily torture.

But even in the worst possible situation, you can deal with it. You have that power. It lies in growing independent of your children's mom. In spite of your anger at your children's mother's new partner, it's important to recognize that he has rights too—just as you have rights if you become involved with a woman with children. He has the right to be treated with some level of respect even when you disagree. He has the right to a relationship with your children's mom as they want it, as long as it does not harm your kids. He has the right to a relationship with your children as long as it is respectful and healthy.

There are many reasons for you to be angry with her new partner. These include loss of control of your children and their mother, the way he treats your children and you, the loneliness of being without your kids, or fear that your children may become even more distant. There's also the important influence of personalities, his, hers, and yours. Some people are just easier to get along with than others. Some folks have a knack for working things out, respecting others, and remaining calm. Some don't.

The role that your children's mother's new partner takes on just by being with her also enters into this equation. His new position with your children's mother gives him responsibilities which he may handle poorly or well. Either way, it's important for you to recognize that the role he's in may affect your conflict with him as much or more than the person he is.

Try not to personalize your dealings with him. Understand the difference between him and the role he occupies. He is in a situation that anyone would have difficulty with, and you'd have at least some trouble getting along with the person in that role no matter who he is.

For your own peace of mind, recognize that there are many things you cannot control about other people no matter how much you want to, and be confident in the fact that you are your children's father. You have more power in your children's lives than any other man. No one can replace you in that role if you intelligently and positively hang in there for the long haul.

One dad I worked with, Luke, was very upset about the way his two children were treated by his former wife's new boyfriend. He felt this man, Dan, was too strict with Luke's children, yet lenient with his own. It upset Luke to see this favoritism, but nothing he did or said made any difference.

Luke came to counseling with his new wife, Sally, at her request. She felt that his anger at Dan was affecting the way he treated her two daughters who lived with them. The situation was truly complicated, with anger, confusion, and blame all around. Still, Luke was a caring father. He wasn't a violent man, and he wanted things to get better.

Luke was direct in telling me that he actively hoped his former wife and Dan would break up. But they weren't breaking up, and, as much as he hated the thought of it, he was starting to realize that they might be together for a long time. It frustrated him to see Dan parenting his sons, but he also began to see that his reactions were making things worse for everyone, so he began to back off from his confrontations with Dan.

By the last counseling session, Luke was confronting Dan much less. Luke and Sally agreed that they were communicating better, that Luke was being less harsh with her daughters, and that tensions between family members had decreased significantly.

In this chapter we have looked at ways to express yourself assertively with your children's mother and her new partner, as well as ways to keep discussions from becoming destructive arguments. The Ten Commandments of Communication can further improve your relationship with your children's mom. It may seem hard to believe that a relationship that ended in divorce or separation can become civil again, but it can, and that civility will clearly improve your relationship with your kids.

CHAPTER 5

Money

"Money doesn't talk, it swears."
—BOB DYLAN

There is never enough money after a divorce. There's no way around it. It takes a lot more money to run two households than one. Division of money and property is a great source of stress for many separating couples and their children who are caught in the middle of arguments over material goods.

Disputes about money are often made worse by child-support laws that don't accurately reflect the costs of raising children or that unfairly divide financial obligations between parents. Additionally, because child-support laws are designed to fit everyone, they often lack the flexibility needed to set fair support awards in individual cases.

Money is important in today's world, but the severity of arguments that so often occur about child support and property division tells us there is more going on. Money conflicts often reflect the powerlessness that separated parents feel. They fight to maintain control of their lives and their money when they feel most threatened. If either parent is obsessed with alcohol, drugs, money, or power, money battles are even more extreme.

During your relationship with your child's mom you both likely struggled with power and control at times, but it was probably much less obvious and angry than it is after a separation. Now, your child's mom—the very person who you rejected or who rejected you—appears to have more power than she did when you were together. She can limit how and when you see your children. She can affect how much money you have for yourself.

Another hidden but powerful influence on arguments live-away dads have today is the insecurity we carry with us from when we were little. Most of us are not aware of that insecurity in our daily adult lives. We may be successful businessmen or community leaders. Other people may look up to us. It is usually only when major power struggles come up in personal relationships that we notice it.

As children we had little control over our lives. This was particularly true through the first eight or so years of our existence, an influential period of life in which self-esteem and the ability to trust are formed. Our emotional state often depended on the decisions of others, and even the best parents could not make our lives completely predictable and secure. That inability to control our own life created insecurities that had an influence over how we felt then—and feel now—about ourselves and the rest of the world. Those long forgotten insecurities sometimes cause us to react much more strongly today than present-day circumstances call for. Under enough pressure, our insecurities surface, and parents attack each other in an attempt to protect themselves and gain control. Once the attack has begun it's very difficult for either parent to cope well with it.

On top of all this, money is supposed to be insignificant compared to our love for our children, still we find ourselves in these money battles. So we struggle with our guilt over focusing so much attention on money when our children are really more important to us. If we don't feel bad enough on our own, society, and sometimes our child's mom, will be glad to remind us how selfish we are. It becomes difficult for parents to have honest conversations about money because they can be interpreted as putting money ahead of children.

Both Parents Are Often Upset About Money

Some live-in moms receive no child support, and many more, correctly or incorrectly, believe that they are not getting enough. At the other extreme, dads often feel, correctly or incorrectly, that they are paying more money than the other parent needs for the children or that the money is being spent poorly.

When parents split up, it may bring out anger, hurt, jealousy, and other emotions that have been held back for years. Combine these stresses with the mistrust that parents feel when going in separate directions, and you have a breeding ground for fights about almost anything. In these circumstances it takes a lot of maturity and selflessness by both parents for things to be worked out peacefully.

The challenges of coparenting after separation are even worse when the father and mother were never married or were in a short-term relationship. In those situations, the woman's announcement that she is having a baby is more likely to result in the administration of blood tests than a joyous celebration.

That dad often does not bond well with his child and, as a result, is more likely to see that child as a financial burden than a life to nurture. Moms feel less committed to those dads. More and more of the energy of those moms goes toward bonding with their children. Less energy goes toward bonding with the child's father or encouraging attachment between father and child. The struggle for resources may then become primary, and money and parenting-time become mixed together in unhealthy ways.

I've seen live-away dads keep contact with their children to a minimum out of fear that seeing them more would result in the live-in mom demanding more money. I've seen dads stop a mom from seeking more child support by threatening to see their children more—or less. I've seen cases of a live-in mom settling for a low level of child support for fear that taking her children's father to court would result in his demanding more time with their kids. I've seen moms threaten to raise child support to discourage a dad from seeing his children more. These ways of handling things are obviously unfair to both parents and children.

In any struggle over money, you have two main choices. You can accept the financial situation that exists, or you can fight to change it. Look at your child-support obligations and see if they are in line with state standards. Unless there is something very unusual about your situation, it is highly unlikely that you will pay less than the norm.

Be careful not to put too much stock in comparisons of your financial payments to the payments that others make. You'll always find someone who pays less or in some other way seems better off than you, and that still wouldn't help your situation.

If you feel that your financial obligations are unfair, you can fight them in court individually or as a member of a group of live-away parents trying to change the broader system. Whichever you do, keep looking at yourself to ensure that your fight is not driven primarily by anger, control, or insecurities.

Consider the effects of court proceedings on your children. If your court fight is fueled by a need for control, you can carry out a lifetime of battles and never gain a thing. Certainly your children are unlikely to benefit. So choose well, and whatever your choice, conduct yourself in a way that makes the lives of you and your children better, not bitter.

Bottom Line: You Can Pay Child Support or Not Pay It

The whole issue of child support is more complex and emotionally painful than many people understand unless they have gone through it themselves. In Wisconsin the standard child-support payment for one child is 17 percent of the live-away parent's income before taxes are subtracted. For two children it is 25 percent. Payments like this can be a real hardship on live-away dads, particularly if they have a new family of their own. To make matters worse, the live-in mom's household income is usually not considered in setting support, and she can spend the child support any way she wants with no oversight by the courts.

Money payments are easy to measure; parenting skills are not. If a father is behind in child support, it's on the record and action can be taken against him. He can have his paychecks garnished, his tax refunds intercepted, and even be thrown in jail. If a mother does a poor job raising her children or wastes the money she receives, little is done about it.

Many times dads are seen as walking wallets, and when they don't pay we see headlines about "deadbeat dads" in the newspapers, a slap in the face of all live-away dads, many of whom are current on child support. We rarely hear about obstruction of parenting-time by unfair mothers.

Nonpayment of child support is a serious problem, and there are far too many fathers who shirk their financial responsibility to their children. But there are also many live-in moms who do poor jobs in parenting their children and who obstruct parenting-time with their children's fathers. It's not only money that counts.

A lot has been done to enforce payment of child support, but little has been done to encourage paternal involvement in parenting. We hear a lot about dads who give up on their children, but little is reported about the millions of loving and involved fathers who support their children beautifully in spite of emotional and financial hardships.

What does all this mean for the dad reading this book? Faced with a financial situation that may be unfair, you are left with choices to make. Once a child support amount has been determined, you are obligated to pay it. It may not be fair. It may not be reasonable. But it has been set. At that point you have two choices. You can pay it or not pay it, and there are consequences for each choice.

One choice is to not pay support. The consequence of that choice may be the deterioration of your relationship with your children and their mother, because it is reasonable for her to expect the full child support that the court has ordered even if it is not a fair amount.

Other consequences of not paying child support include tax intercepts, the long-term accumulation of debt, high attorney fees, and increased battles between parents. All of these consequences are unpleasant, and to my mind are worse than paying the support. I would encourage parents who are not paying their support to ask themselves why they don't. Child-support payments create a financial burden for live-away parents, and in some cases they simply cannot afford it, but considering all the negative consequences of not paying, it is fair to ask if, for some dads, nonpayment has moved beyond a financial struggle and become a way to say, "You can't make me."

Choice number two is to pay the full support. Regular and full payment of child support will often improve your access to your children because their mom will be more likely to cooperate with you. Full payment keeps the government off your back. Also, if you are current in your child-support payments, you will be taken more seriously by court personnel any time you bring parenting-time matters before them.

Your children deserve your financial support for expenses such as food, rent or house payments, utilities, transportation, school supplies, clothes, personal items, and many other things. Even cases in which their mother spends money in ways you dislike, your payments do have some positive impact on your children's situation. It may help you to think of your support as going to your children's needs and any other income their mom has as going to things you don't approve of.

Why One Dad Paid His Full Child Support

There are several reasons why I was always up to date with my child support for the twelve years that my daughters lived with their mother. I didn't do it because I was rich, to be a hero, or to be a martyr. I did it because I saw no better choices.

For years I considered my twice-a-month payments to be ransom, not child support. I didn't like the way my former wife raised our daughters or spent my money. For years I lived in small apartments while she, her new husband, and my daughters lived in a big, expensive home.

I thought a lot about not paying, but I knew that if I stopped, I'd have more trouble seeing my kids than I already was. I thought about stalling payments, making small payments, missing payments, claiming hardships, or switching jobs to get out of paying, but I also knew that every time I went back to court to fight, the lawyers were the ones that got my money.

There were lots of hard times. Once I was laid off for several months and got my support reduced to 25 percent of the minimum wage until I got a new job. It didn't leave me much to live on. A couple of years after my divorce I quit my job to finish graduate school full-time. During that year or so I didn't miss any child-support payments or even attempt to have them lowered. I worked part-time and took out enough school loans to continue payments through that period. I didn't ask for a decrease in child support because it was my decision to go back to college, and I didn't think the courts would allow a reduction. I decided to just work it out. I don't like owing money to anybody. I knew that if I got behind in payments they would just build up and strangle me some time in the future. I didn't want that stone around my neck.

I also kept up because it helped provide for my daughters' basic needs of food, clothes, a place to live, and other things they needed. To be honest with you, I don't think a lot of my money really went toward their needs, but some did. My job was to send it. My former wife's job was to spend it, and I knew that wasn't going to change.

One of the biggest reasons I paid all my support was that it calmed down my former wife, which made things easier on my daughters. When she was mad at me it was hard for anyone to be around her, especially our daughters. I didn't want them to go through that, so I did my best to keep things level.

I've never really doubted that I did the right thing. I'm sure it made life much easier for my daughters and me. They are doing well now as young women, and we are very close. I don't think it would have worked out as well if I had constantly fought with their mother about child support.

CHAPTER 6

Is My Children's Mother Harming Our Kids?

"I cannot think of any need in childhood as strong as the need for a father's protection."
—SIGMUND FREUD

As a live-away dad, there may be times when you are extremely worried about the care your former partner is giving your children. For many dads this worry is constant. But even when you feel the worst—and are most convinced that she is harming the kids—you *might* be mistaken, and that could be unfortunate for your children and you.

Exaggerated assessments of harm can lead to increased anger between parents and leave you unable to deal with your kids or their mother in a calm and positive way. On the other hand, underestimation of harm may subject your children to ongoing maltreatment that could be stopped. For these reasons, it is very important that you accurately assess what happens to your kids.

Factors That Interfere with Accurate Assessment of Harm

There are several factors that make it difficult to determine whether your children's mother is harming your kids. The first three factors are inaccurate information, mistrust of the other parent, and difficulty looking closely at yourself. The fourth influence, already discussed in chapter 1, is the extreme emotional pain that parents go through during and after a breakup. Let's look now at the first three factors one at a time.

1. Inaccurate information

When live-away dads and live-in moms get into fights about how their children are treated, inaccurate information usually has much to do with it. Because of the communication problems that are created and magnified by the ending of a relationship, information does not get properly checked out, and arguments result.

I worked with Tom and Alice when I was a court mediator. These parents were never married but had lived together, and a couple years after they moved apart, Tom requested mediation because he wanted more time with his daughter. Alice opposed it, but because the mediation was court ordered, she was required to attend.

During the first joint mediation session Alice brought up an incident that had greatly upset her. She stated that their six-year-old daughter, Judy, had told her of a time, several weeks earlier, when Tom angrily pushed her head into the water of the toilet. Alice did not trust Tom's care of Judy in the first place and saw this incident as proof of how uncontrollable Tom got when he was upset.

Because of the poor communication between these parents, Alice had never asked Tom what happened. When she finally brought this incident up in mediation, Tom was angry about her accusation and responded with a totally different version of what had happened. He said that Judy had been sick that weekend (which Alice acknowledged was true). He went on to say that at one point he and his girlfriend were in the bathroom with Judy as she threw up in the toilet. Her hair started to fall forward into the water, and Tom grabbed it to keep her dry. After Judy was done being sick, they put her to bed. He denied being angry at his daughter or mistreating her in any way.

As both parents told their stories, the tension in the room lessened. For the first time they were actually talking together about what had happened. After much discussion, Alice came to accept Tom's version of what had occurred. This led to improved communication and cooperation on other issues.

I worked with Alice and Tom for several sessions. My sense was that they both cared a great deal about their daughter and were capable parents. How, then, could such wildly different stories come about? If Tom didn't push his daughter's head into the toilet, why did Alice say he did? Is Alice a liar? Is Tom a liar? Is six-year-old Judy a liar? Did Alice manipulate her daughter into saying this to stop Tom from seeing Judy?

I am convinced no one in this story was a liar or manipulator. To me it was an example of two caring parents in great distress. Both were telling the truth *as they knew it*, but emotional pain and inaccurate information got in the way.

Two forms of inaccurate information

Inaccurate information comes in two forms—intentionally inaccurate and unintentionally inaccurate, in other words, a lie or a mistake. The great majority of inaccurate information I hear in discussions between separated parents is a mistake, yet mistrusting parents usually think it's a lie, and the stronger the conflict between parents, the more likely they are to think that the other parent is being dishonest. In the extreme, all mistakes are assumed to be lies. Dishonesty may increase in the most hostile separations, but I am sure that each parent's belief that the other parent is lying goes up even more.

Sources of inaccurate information

Inaccurate information comes from a variety of sources, including people you dislike, friends and relatives, your child's mom, and your children. They may not tell you everything about everything because of a legitimate fear that sharing information with you betrays the other parent, creates bigger problems, or puts the kids in the middle. It may even be difficult for them to tell you good things about your former partner if you let it be known by your words or actions that you don't want to hear them. If your re-actions are too negative, people face the "kill the messenger" dilemma, that you will be angry at them for delivering a message you don't want to hear.

Children are frequently a source of inaccurate information about their lives. Be very careful not to automatically believe what they tell you. They may be telling the truth, but they often make mistakes in describing what happens around them. It was a common experience in my parenting-time mediation sessions and custody evaluations to see parents completely outraged over incidents they learned about through their children only to find out later that things had not happened at all as described.

Children are in the middle. If parents are angry at each other, it is particularly difficult for kids to talk accurately about what happened with one parent or the other. When describing what happened in an incident they often tell what a parent did to them—but not what they did that led to that parent's actions. They also may minimize or exaggerate events without realizing it. They may overstate things due to their emotional state. Rarely, however, are they lying. Children, even teenagers, are simply too young, vulnerable, and emotionally involved to describe events precisely.

We have different definitions for words

Another reason information may be inaccurate is that people often interpret words differently. Let's use the example of "yelling." I hear many parents accuse their former partners of yelling at their children. But what is yelling? How do you define it? Is it how harshly the words are said? Is it a matter of which words are used? How loud the words are spoken? How long it goes on? How high or low the voice is?

When I was a juvenile court social worker I had a teenage girl on my caseload named Colette. This young lady had been placed under six months' supervision for running away from home. During my first visit to Colette's home, I sat with her and the rest of her family at the dining room table. I happened to sit between

Colette and her father and quickly noticed how loud and harsh his speech was.

At one point in our conversation I turned to Colette and asked, "Does your dad ever yell at you?" Her response was, "No, hardly ever." I was shocked. In my opinion, he was yelling while we sat at the table. Colette might have said he didn't yell because she was afraid to anger her dad, but I didn't think so. She never seemed afraid to speak up in front of her parents and, in fact, her frequent challenges to them were one of the struggles in this family.

When Colette told me her dad didn't yell I turned to him and said, "Well, I thought you were yelling quite a bit right here." I went on to explain that when I was a child, angry or loud words were rarely used by my parents, and that the exchange I heard in his dining room would clearly be considered yelling in my family.

It became clear to me that Colette's dad probably raised his voice in anger very often but that neither he nor his family saw it that way. Though yelling in this family had probably contributed to Colette running away, no one was aware of it. After they became more conscious of this communication problem and others and worked to improve on how they expressed themselves, some of Colette's problems improved as well.

Words can have very different meanings to different people. Don't jump to conclusions when you hear things, and if you are unsure of what someone means, ask for clarification. When in doubt, check it out.

Definitions versus labels

One way to improve communication is to *define* behavior rather than *label* it. "Yelling" is an example of a label, a quick method of classifying an action. Labels are often loaded with value judgments and may have as many definitions as there are people. On the other hand, definitions provide an opportunity for shared understanding. Let's look at an example of defining versus labeling.

A teenager, Joanna, lives with her mom after her parents are separated. She complains to her mother that her dad yells at her for talking on the phone too long. Her story to her mom might be something like this: "I was on the phone last night, and dad started yelling at me again. I hardly had a chance to talk and he started in."

If mom talks to dad about this "yelling" incident, he can respond to her with either a conversation that *labels* or one that *defines*. A labeling conversation may go something like this:

Mom says, "Joanna told me you were yelling at her again last night. Can't you try to stay calmer with her?"

Dad responds, "I didn't yell at her. You know she exaggerates, and whenever she blames me for something you instantly take her side."

"No, I don't," says mom. "I just know what you are like with her."

"How can you know what I am like with her?" replies dad. "You weren't even there. You're the one who never disciplines her. If you'd do that once in a while, we wouldn't have these problems."

As things continue to heat up, mom says, "Well, there you go again, blaming me when you can't handle her . . ."

And the fight goes on. Nobody really communicates. Both parents just defend and attack. But many of these arguments could be avoided by staying on the point and calmly but assertively explaining exactly what happened. A defining conversation might go like this:

Mom says, "Joanna told me you were yelling at her again last night. Can't you try to stay calmer with her?"

Dad responds with, "I didn't yell at her. She had been on the phone for nearly an hour even though I asked her several times to get off. I did raise my voice, but I didn't lose my temper, call her names, or threaten her."

Mom answers with, "Well, that's not what she said. She told me you were screaming at her after she had been on the phone for just a few minutes."

"That's not what happened," says dad. "I didn't scream. I was firm with my voice, but sometimes she doesn't pay attention until I do that. I looked at the clock several times that night, and I know she was on the phone for at least forty-five minutes. I insisted that she get off the phone, but I stayed calm throughout the time I was dealing with this."

As dad explains what happened, mom begins to trust him a bit and says, "I sure hope so. I know she exaggerates a lot, but she was very upset about what happened."

Because things are staying calm, dad is able to say, "I under-stand that. I care about her too, but I think I have to set limits with her. I appreciate you telling me what she said so we could talk about this."

In this example, parents are communicating. Dad responds to accusations of "yelling" by explaining his view of what actually happened. He stays calm and defines his behavior rather than get-ting caught in an argument. Both parents are then able to stay on the subject. There still may be different opinions of what occurred, but things don't get out of hand.

2. Mistrust of the other parent

Mistrust of a former partner is another thing that makes it difficult to accurately assess possible harm to your children. Trust-building is difficult in the best of times; after separation it often seems im-possible. In many ways, the ending of an intense relationship is the ultimate break in trust, and it's difficult to communicate and work with someone we don't trust.

But mistrust is complicated, and, in fact, our mistrust after a re-lationship ends is greatly influenced by something that has nothing to do with our former partner—broken bonds. A mutual bond is crucial to healthy trust between two adults. Through a divorce or other breakup, that bond is often broken. Without that mutual bond and commitment, parents strike out on their own separate paths.

I visualize healthy bonds between parents as two clasped hands with fingers intertwined and palms together. There is strength and connection there. It takes a lot of force to separate those interlock-ing fingers. If, however, one or both hands pull away with enough force, the bond will be broken. The hands will be separated. What used to be two hands joined together by mutual goals—no matter how imperfect—becomes two fists with separate goals. If the separation is violent enough, those fists end up smashing into each other. The relationship changes from being *cooperative* to having to be *right*.

Your mistrust of a former partner may be justified, but you must also recognize that mistrust does affect your ability to assess harm accurately.

3. Difficulty looking closely at yourself

By looking at your own mistakes as well as those of your child's mom, you are better able to assess harm accurately. It's often very difficult to look at your own role in parenting conflicts that come up. It's hard to remain calm and objective. But by looking closely at your own mistakes, you make better decisions, and there's less tension between parents. Just as a salesman must know his strengths and weaknesses to build a favorable relationship with a customer, you must know your strengths and weaknesses to build a working relationship with your child's mom.

Self-examination requires conscious effort. You can't just hope things will change. You must pay careful attention to how you deal with conflicts with your child's mother and consciously look for ways to improve your own actions. One thing that will help you with this is motivation, the desire to feel better day in and day out and to have a better relationship with your child. Use that motivation to remind you of the importance of conscious effort. Brutal honesty about yourself is also an important ingredient in assessing harm accurately. It gives you the gift of seeing your own mistakes. We all make them. Successful people are the ones who know what their mistakes are and look to improve on them.

Many live-away dads worry a great deal about the parenting that their children's moms carry out. I hope this section has given you some tools to use in evaluating possible mistreatment of your children. Looking closely at yourself, understanding the effects of mistrust of your children's mom, and using accurate information when assessing potential harm to your children will allow you to decide with more confidence whether your children are being harmed by their mom.

Now let's look at constructive ways to respond to parenting decisions that your former partner may make.

Turning Harm into Help

As a court mediator and custody evaluator, I was often required to assess harm to children. One way I tried to do so was to ask myself, "Which does the greater harm to a child, the parenting decisions made by one parent or the reactions to those decisions by the other parent?" Look closely at that question yourself.

Your children can be harmed or helped by their mom's parenting decisions, and they can be harmed or helped by how you react to those decisions or to her in general. If you are upset with what's happening, deal with that frustration with a friend, counselor, support group, relatives, or the courts, but be sure that you don't overreact with your children or their mother and complicate things even more.

Known versus unknown behaviors

I think we sometimes fool ourselves. We say we are trying to work things out with our child's mother, but we don't always act that way. One way we fool ourselves is to apply one parenting measure to her—what we think she did or what she probably did—and another measure to ourselves, the mistakes we have actually been caught in. We let ourselves off the hook by using these different measurements.

One dad I worked with, Barry, illustrates this point well. He was divorced for the second time in his late thirties. He had an eight-year-old daughter, Cassandra, from that marriage. He and Cassandra's mother, Patty, had separated when their daughter was only two years old and Barry worked hard to stay close to her through the years.

It seemed to Barry that Patty was jealous of his relationship with Cassandra. Patty intentionally planned appointments or school activities when he was supposed to be with his daughter. She also made decisions about child care, her own dating life, and other things that he greatly disagreed with.

Barry was often angry and upset with Patty's parenting. In his words, "I just about went nuts over things she was doing. What frustrated me even more than that was the fact that no matter what I said or how I said it, she never listened."

After years of butting his head against this brick wall, Barry began to accept something. He couldn't change Patty. He began to see that he would have to work on himself if things were going to change. "What generated the best results for me," he said, "was to look objectively at my own behavior and weaknesses when I got mad at her. At first I looked just at my surface behavior. Things that were known to her or other people. But after a while I realized that I also had to look at my behavior that other people didn't know about.

"There were plenty of dumb things I'd done over the years to remind me that Patty wasn't the only one that made mistakes. I got mad too often at Patty and my daughter. Patty and I sometimes argued in front of Cassandra in person and on the phone. I was a heavy drinker for several years, and I know I did lots of dumb things then, but these were all things that Patty knew about. To stop myself from going nuts and to be fair to my daughter, I also had to think of the things I did that people didn't know about."

Barry then told me a story of a poor judgment he had made once, one that Patty never knew about. It was not a major incident, but it had the potential to be.

"Cassandra stayed with me for a couple weeks every summer, and one year just after I had moved into a new house, and she was about eight years old, she wrote a letter to her mom and wanted to mail it herself. I was a little concerned that she might not be able to find the mailbox, which was past an angle street at the far corner of the block, but I figured it would be okay and sent her off.

"She didn't return after a few minutes, and I started to get a little nervous. Pretty soon I realized that she was taking too long for sure, so I got in my car and drove off to get her. I got to the mailbox just in time to see my daughter getting into a cop car! I didn't know what would happen next.

"Well, the cop turned out to be a nice guy. I thanked him and took Cassandra home. She wasn't scared at all and was only sad that she couldn't ride in the police car. On the way home I asked her what happened. She told me that she had mailed the letter but then got lost. At that point she went up to a house, knocked on the door, and asked for help. Luckily it was the home of a nice elderly couple. They couldn't locate me by phone or bring Cassandra home because I had just moved there. I wasn't listed in the phone book or directory assistance, and Cassandra didn't know the address or phone number.

"I never did tell Patty what happened. I was afraid that she might try to use it against me some time in the future if we ever get into battles about custody or visitation. To tell the truth, I would probably try to use it against her if she did anything like that.

"The problem is, she didn't do it, I did. It helps me to remember that when I get mad at her. Few people knew about what happened. But I do. So now when I get really pissed at Patty I try to remember all the mistakes I made with our daughter—not just the ones Patty knows about. It cools me down a lot to remind myself of that."

Actual harm versus potential harm

In the mailbox incident there was no actual harm to Barry's daughter, but the potential was great. Images of Cassandra being kidnapped had confronted Barry as he had driven off to look for her. That's what scared him and what would have outraged him had something like this happened under Patty's care.

Barry told me, "As I thought about what happened, I realized something. When I made mistakes I just looked at what actually happened. When Patty made mistakes I reacted to what could have happened at the worst. The potential harm of what could have happened was always greater, of course. When I looked at things that way, Patty always looked worse."

Honesty without attack

When you accurately assess what happens with your former partner, you are more likely to deal with her in a way that I call honesty without attack. Honesty without attack means standing up for yourself and saying what you need to say—without blasting people. Honesty without attack allows you to take your masculine power and use it in strong, caring, and healing ways. It's done legally and openly, with full explanation. It is a commitment to work with your children's mom for the sake of the kids—even when she does not work well with you—because divorce or separation has not lessened the importance of your commitment to your children. It has only changed its form.

Use your masculine power to make things better, and remember that the power you have lies in changing yourself, not others. Believing that you have the right or power to change someone else can be an alluring trap, one that will only end in frustration. Expecting your child's mom to do what you think she should—especially when you are absolutely positive that your idea is the best thing to do—is a recipe for disaster. It's a disaster because it requires her to change what you think she should, rather than her deciding freely with you what—or if—she wants to change.

If you find yourself frustrated because your child's mom is not keeping up with her end of the agreements you've made, remind yourself that you can't change her. If she doesn't follow through on what she said she'd do—whatever the reason—that is her decision. You have once again found yourself in a position where you cannot change her regardless of how important it is, how much you want it, or what she's said she'd do.

If the two of you are able to cooperate with each other, communicate fairly well, and both work hard on making change, it makes sense for you to work together. But that's not you trying to change you and her. It's you trying to change you, and her trying to change her.

Ironically, when you stop trying to change your child's mom, she's more likely to change herself because then it's her decision. You must make changes in your behavior because they are the best thing to do—not in the hopes that she will see what you've done and change herself. That's simply another example of trying to change her.

When things get tough between you and your child's mom, it is easy to lose your cool, to say or do things that make problems for you and your child. Be aware of when you are stepping over the line from *telling* your child's mom what you want—to *demanding* that she do it. Demanding things from her drains you. Your energy is wasted on a nearly impossible task.

One way to avoid demanding that she do things your way is to see that you do not swear, yell, call names, use physical force of any kind, or give the cold shoulder. These are all aggressive acts that will only hurt your relationship with her (or, for that matter, anyone else you use them on). If you catch yourself doing any of these things, stop yourself, get away to cool down if you need to, and continue the conversation later.

You have every right to be angry, frustrated, upset, scared, or hurt if things are not going the way you'd like. You don't, however, have a right to use aggressive language or actions against others. Those aggressive acts will only make things worse. Instead of using these demanding styles of communication, do your best to be assertive but calm in getting what you want.

It may be difficult for you to avoid demands—especially if your former partner is equally or more demanding herself. But what she does is not the point. This book is not about changing her. She's not reading it. It is about you changing *you*. That you can always do, and that's where your power lies.

Helpful Communication

Men can be excellent communicators, but when we get off base, we often do so in one of two ways. One is to say nothing, and the other is to make angry demands. Sometimes we do both. We clam up and hold our anger in as long as we can until we finally blow up. We don't speak up because we don't want to start an argument, we think the other person should know what we want, or we are afraid we'll blow up. This pattern not only harms communication, but it can lead to sleepless nights, ulcers, or bouts of temper followed by guilt.

Most people will acknowledge that clamming up or blowing up is not helpful, but they don't quite know what to do instead. Some think the other person just isn't listening right. I've had dads in marriage counseling say to me, "We've been married twenty years. I don't have to tell her how I feel. She should know what I want."

My response to that is that she does need to hear from you directly. Not telling her what you want lets her know something is wrong, but it doesn't tell her what it is. She can't read your mind, so tell her in words what you are thinking and feeling. You don't have to say everything just right, but try to express yourself calmly and completely. The following three-part method can be very helpful.

First, state *how you feel*, then tell her *what you are upset about*, and finally, tell her *what you would like*. She may do some, all, or none of what you want, but at least you asked! At least you expressed what is bothering you and what you want. That in itself is a great release. At the best you'll get what you want, and at the least you won't walk away saying, "Damn, I wish I would have told her . . ."

Here is an example of harmful and helpful communication between divorced parents about their children; Jessica and Ryan. Notice the difference between them.

Harmful Bill to Jane: "How can you let Jessica constantly get away with not doing homework? It's unbelievable! You know she needs to study every night to keep up. I've asked you a hundred times to get her to do it, but you never do. Your sister even thinks you're too easy on Jessica! Just make her do her homework. You should think more about her and less about yourself!"

Helpful Bill to Jane: "I want you to know I am really upset and worried about Jessica [how you feel—upset and worried]. She is not keeping up with her classes [what you are concerned about], and I am asking you to try to get her to study more regularly [what you want]."

Here is another example.

Harmful Bill to Jane: "I found out that Ryan got a speeding ticket last week and you did nothing about it. You still let him drive. You constantly give in to him and let him do whatever he wants! You never say 'no' to him. Why don't you, for once in your life, punish him. He's walking all over you. It's obvious as hell he'll get more tickets when you do nothing about it."

Helpful Bill to Jane: "I am very concerned about something [how you feel—concerned]. Ryan just told me he got a speeding ticket, yet you still let him drive. I think he's going to get into more trouble if he is not disciplined more [what you are concerned about]. I think he should not be able to drive the car for at least two weeks. I would like us to agree on some consequence and enforce it together [what you would like]."

Saying what we want is not to be confused with getting what we want, but they are related. Jane may disagree with what Bill sees as the problem and the solution, but at least presenting it in a calm and constructive way is a start to better communication.

Calm and nonblaming communication has another huge advantage. Even when compromise cannot be reached, there is an opportunity to get more accurate information about what occurred. Because Jane is not being attacked, there is a better chance she will talk with Bill about what happened.

In the harmful examples above, Bill made lots of assumptions without checking them out with Jane. It's possible that Jane actually agrees with him about Jessica's homework. She might even want Bill's help in getting Jessica to do it, but she's not very likely to admit that if he's blaming her for the problem.

In the situation with Ryan, maybe Ryan didn't tell the whole story to his dad, or maybe there are other problems going on in relation to his driving. It's possible that Jane would truly like Bill's help but is afraid to bring up problems because of how their conversations go.

The harmful examples above are very blaming, and Bill talks mainly about Jane. Notice how many times the word "you" is used. Sentences like that are sometimes referred to as "you messages." They are always about the other person and her behavior. They are often negative and attacking, and they frequently lead to counterattack or withdrawal by the other person.

The harmful examples also make predictions of future events, use swearing, and make assumptions ("It's obvious as hell he'll get more tickets when you do nothing about it."). They also tell the listener what to do ("Just make her do her homework." "Take the car away for at least two weeks."). Bill talks a lot more about Jane than himself, and there is no sense of compromise, no listening.

The helpful examples are different. They feel less threatening, and Bill is talking primarily about himself, not Jane. Upset, worry, and concern are expressed honestly to let Jane know how he feels, but Jane is not blamed for this and Bill is not out of control.

Notice how many times the word "I" is used in the helpful examples. In these "I statements" the speaker tells about himself, how he feels, why he's upset, and what he wants. Some of us were raised to think it's selfish to talk about ourselves, but the opposite is true. Effective communication requires us to talk about ourselves. If we don't, how are others going to know about us? Talking about ourselves is not bragging or selfish. It's honest communication that lessens arguments by taking the focus off others.

The helpful examples above express how Bill feels, what he's upset about, and what he wants. This is much less threatening to others than telling them what they did wrong or what they should do. Try this three-part method and "I statements" in your communication. They take practice, but over time they can definitely improve how you communicate.

Change Takes Effort, But Stick with It

Today's society emphasizes the quick fix administered painlessly. Drug companies compete over whose pill rids you of your headache the fastest. If it takes a whole minute to end a stomach-ache, it's too long. Everything from cleaning your stove to replacing all your body fat with rippling muscle is the easiest thing in the world. You don't have to do the work. The product does it for you instantly, with no effort, odor, or scrubbing.

Unfortunately, real change isn't like that. All problems are not resolved beautifully in thirty minutes minus commercial breaks. So don't get down on yourself if change doesn't come as quickly or easily as you'd like. The quick fix isn't real. A steady and determined commitment to make things work out with your children is.

CHAPTER 7

Communicating with Your New Partner and Others

"Getting people to like you is merely the other side of liking them."
—NORMAN VINCENT PEALE

There are others who affect your relationship with your children besides their mother. In this chapter, you'll get ideas on how to work cooperatively with your new partner and other people in your children's lives, including your children's grandparents, other adults, and stepchildren.

To get started, write the names of your live-away children in the middle of a large piece of paper. Now draw a big circle around them, and on that circle, write the names of five to ten of the most important and influential living people in their lives. Include anyone who has a strong influence on them whether you get along with that person or not.

Who is on that circle? Certainly you are there, as is their mother. Others might include their grandparents, possibly a step-parent or stepbrother or stepsister, other relatives, siblings, you or your former wife's closest friends, your new partner, an important teacher or coach. Anyone else? If so, put them around the circle.

Now do the same thing for yourself. Who is on your circle of influence (positive or negative)? Your children, your parents, siblings, a good friend, your former partner, a new partner if you have one? Anyone else? Put them on that circle.

Now take a moment to think about the ways that people in either circle influence your children or you. How powerful is that influence? How helpful is it? Are there any things you could do to make that influence more positive?

Now make a separate list of the people whose names appear on both circles. You have just identified the folks who are probably most important to your relationship with your children. The better you get along with them, the better it is for your children—and for you. Seek the support of the people you trust on those circles. If there are people that you don't get along with, think of at least one thing you could do to improve your relationship with each of them. Within the next week, do at least one of those things.

Your New Partner

If you have a current wife or girlfriend, she may be angry at your child's mom, get along with her well, feel sorry for her, be jealous, or all of the above at different times. She may feel in the middle between you and your child's mom, and she probably wonders at times what her role is with your child.

You and your current partner may struggle with many things. How do you balance your different parenting styles (discipline, communication, guidance, openness)? If she brings children to your relationship, how do you deal with them? How do the two of you handle communication with former partners? How do you deal with child support? How do you blend family traditions, customs, and rules from different homes? How do you muster the energy—or even the time—to give your children the individual attention they need?

These challenges can weigh heavily on your new relationship. That's why it's so important to work together on problems that come up. If you lock her out of the struggles you're having—or put too much responsibility on her to solve them—you harm your relationship with her.

Research shows that married couples that stay together have

about the same number and types of problems (deaths, job losses, illnesses, money issues, etc.) as married couples that don't stay together. The difference between them is that the ones that stay together communicate about those problems. To be one of the families that stays together, it may help you to use the SHARE approach to relationships. The letters of the word SHARE represent five important qualities to help you communicate with your new partner and others:

Shared communication
Honesty
Adjustment
Responsibility
Effort

Shared communication is crucial in your relationship with your new partner. Let her know what you want for yourself, for her, her children if she has any, your children, and your children's mother. Talk about how both of you will get what you want. Come to joint decisions.

The most important part of shared communication is what I call "enhanced listening." Listen to what your partner wants, feels, and thinks without attempts to control, direct, or persuade her. Just listen. Give her your undivided attention. If, as she's talking, you find yourself thinking about what your response to her is going to be—stop it! You can't listen to her and plan your strategies at the same time. Conversations are most productive when they serve as opportunities to know each other better, not a contest to see who's right.

I once had a conversation with a mom who argued a lot with her long-term boyfriend. I asked her how she defined communication. She told me it was "getting him to understand what I'm trying to say." I tried to help her see that both of them listening to each other might be a better definition.

The best arguments imaginable—presented by the world's greatest orator—won't get through to someone who isn't listening.

If life were a football game, both of you listening would be like a Superbowl victory. One of you listening would be like an overtime loss. Neither of you listening would be like somebody barricading the locker-room door so you couldn't get onto the field.

Honesty is a vital ingredient in the relationship mix. Honesty is about telling the truth, but it's more than that. It's about telling the whole truth—not just the part that's easiest.

I once worked with a dad, Fred, who told me how angry he was at his child's mom for not having their son home when he went to pick him up for the night. As I talked to him in detail, however, he admitted that he had not been completely sure of the pick-up arrangements. He said, "Because I don't want to talk to Nancy any more than I absolutely have to, I never confirmed exactly when I was supposed to pick up my son. I thought the pick-up time was four P.M. and when I got there she said it was six P.M. I was really pissed off, but to tell you the truth, she might have been right. I had just gone ahead and hoped I was right."

It took me a while to get Fred to acknowledge his part in this mix-up (okay, I had to drag it out of him), but after he finally did, it was a relief to him. Acknowledging his part of the problem helped him see that he could get better results in the future by changing what *he* did.

After that, Fred was much clearer about pick-up arrangements for his son. In all future discussions about exchange times, Fred repeated to Nancy exactly what he thought they'd agreed on before he left the house or got off the phone. He even got into the habit of writing down the next pick-up time so he wouldn't forget it, and in the beginning he gave a copy to her. Arguments and misunderstandings about the pick-up time ended.

Honesty with your partner requires honesty with yourself. If you are upset about something your child's mom or your new partner does, acknowledge it to yourself and share it with your partner. Talking about your frustration lets her know what's going on with you and helps you work through it.

Adjustment means responding, in a flexible way, to the huge variety of changes that happen in life, whether they are rain showers that put a stop to a previously planned picnic or your teenager canceling his time with you at the last minute to attend a rock concert with friends. Your ability to adjust well allows you, and all the people around you, to benefit from those inevitable changes in life, rather than sullenly suffer through them.

Adjustment begins with recognition. Be aware of changes around you; don't miss them because you're too busy to notice. Don't dismiss them because they aren't as important to you as they are to others. Don't ignore them because you think they shouldn't happen. After recognition comes response. Do something about the changes, hopefully something positive. Recognize and respond positively to changes, because they happen whether you want them to or not. You might as well make those changes turn into something good.

Responsibility means not faulting others for what's happening to you and not expecting others to fix it. Your current (or future) partner probably wants to be there for you in parenting, so seek her support, and give support to her, but don't put the primary responsibility of dealing with your kids or their mother on her.

In my work with people I have noticed that they often fall into similar patterns of behavior in one relationship after another. See if you find patterns in how you relate to women in your life. If you recognize any behaviors on your part that are not healthy, work on changing them. When you take on that responsibility, relationships flourish.

Effort changes what we want into what we get. The SHARE technique means little without it. It takes effort to channel frustration, overcome loneliness, handle financial hardships, fully appreciate our kids, and communicate well with our new partners. Fortunately, the rewards of this effort are great.

I know a live-away dad, Louis, who has an amazing ability to use SHARE techniques with Gina, his live-in girlfriend of two years. Divorced for seven years, he works hard to stay close to his teenage daughter but not too close to her mother, Sadie, because sometimes he still finds himself attracted to her.

Louis knows, for the million reasons they got divorced, that going back to Sadie would not be a good move, but he still finds himself wanting her. He's even told Gina about his attraction to Sadie. It's been hard for him to be this open, but he felt he had to if there was going to be trust between Gina and him, so he's employed the SHARE techniques to help him handle it.

He uses *shared communication* with Gina and talks *honestly* about the conflicted feelings he's had about Sadie. He's told me that when he tells Gina about how he sometimes feels toward Sadie it's like a great weight is lifted off his shoulders. Because he's so open about it, she trusts him, and he doesn't feel like he's keeping a secret. Louis *adjusts* well and reacts calmly to circumstances that come up with Gina, his daughter, and Sadie, and he takes *responsibility* for his own actions, including how he deals with Sadie. He puts a lot of *effort* into his relationship with Gina because he wants to keep that healthy relationship going.

Using the SHARE technique helps Louis, and it can help you too. Getting along with your new partner while facing the challenge of living away from your children requires shared communication, honesty with yourself and others, adjustment to changing circumstances, responsibility for your actions, and effort to make things work.

Grandparents

Grandparents deserve special consideration. Whether they are your parents or your former partner's parents, their influence in the lives of your children is powerful and important. Grandparents are usually very emotionally connected to their grandchildren and are a meaningful source of support and love for them.

The sense of kinship that grandparents add to the lives of your children is immeasurable. The wisdom that comes from their life experiences is a gift. Grandparents are a connection with family elders and ancestors that grounds children and provides them with a deep connection to their family and its history.

Grandparents are often able to separate themselves from the

struggles of their children and serve as a stabilizing influence in the lives of their grandchildren at a time when they need it the most. It is important for parents to recognize the vital role that grandparents play in the lives of their children and strongly support that meaningful intergenerational contact.

Unfortunately, wounded parents sometimes don't understand the importance of grandparents and try to exclude them from their children's lives. This is particularly true with angry live-in moms who sometimes attempt to minimize contact by their children's father or his family, even at the expense of their children. This can be extremely painful to grandparents who may have intimate connections to their grandchildren one day and be cut off from them the next. In a way, they are like their grandchildren—thrust into the middle of a battle they did not choose.

Fortunately, all fifty states have passed some form of grandparent visitation laws (what I call parenting-time laws), and all states have laws that allow them to seek custody of their grandchildren. However, obtaining the right to see grandchildren is often hard, and winning a custody battle is even more difficult, but cases can be won, and these legal rights that grandparents hold can be very important to children.

As much as grandparents love their children and grandchildren, they can be difficult to deal with themselves at times. They may not understand the legal limitations you face as a live-away dad or the other social and emotional problems you struggle with. They may give advice you don't want or can't do anything about.

If grandparents make suggestions that you disagree with, tell them in a caring and direct way that you appreciate their sincere interest but you have to make your own decisions. Let them know you are doing the best you can. Be sure to tell them how much you appreciate their concern. Point out the things they have done that have helped, and reassure them that you understand how much your children mean to them.

If unrequested advice continues to come your way, set clear limits on what you are willing to discuss and what you aren't. Do your best to keep lines of communication open, however, and do your best to see that conflicts don't interfere with your parents' relationship with you or your children.

Getting along with your former partner's parents can be particularly difficult. I've had several live-away dads tell me that their former in-laws had far too much influence over their daughters. They said those grandparents took their daughters' sides too often, interfered in the dads' parenting, or even encouraged their daughters to leave the dads. Grandparents have told me in response that they were only doing what they thought was right for their daughters and grandchildren.

It's difficult to tell which side is correct when parents and grandparents disagree. Usually both have valid points. Once again we come back to trying to resolve problems as well as possible under difficult circumstances because there is little to be gained by fighting or withdrawing. Understand the dilemma grandparents face, be patient with the struggles your child's grandparents may be going through, and appreciate the support they can provide to you.

Other Adults

It is critical that you maintain positive contact with your children's teachers, friends, relatives, and neighbors whenever possible. If they see you as a reasonable person who loves his children and tries to do well, it will positively influence how they talk about you to your children and your children's mother.

Other adults are not as close to your children as you are, but they may have a lot of influence over you. These people can provide you with support, or they may give you advice that isn't helpful like "Jim, you can't let your kids treat you like this. They never appreciate what you're doing, and their mother is worse. You can't let her get away with changing plans at the last minute all the time. Don't just sit back and let her decide everything. They're your kids too, you know. Give her a piece of your mind and take charge."

You may hear other negative advice like "Thomas, there's nothing more you can do. You've fought your ex for years, and she never changes. If I were you, I'd stop killing myself over those kids. Stop fighting a losing battle. Don't waste your time seeing those kids anymore."

These frustrated advice givers don't understand your love for your children or the limits you face, and, as a result, you may get into arguments with them, clam up, feel like a failure, or doubt yourself. Don't allow their negative advice to get you down. Don't allow it to stop you from seeing your children. Have confidence in your view of the situation. Don't be pressured into taking actions that you are fairly certain will not work. If you aren't sure about the advice you are given, ask for feedback from attorneys or other professionals, positive friends and relatives, or other supportive live-away dads.

A father I worked with years ago, Carlos, had several family members, particularly a sister-in-law, Julia, who couldn't stand how Carlos's former girlfriend, Emma, treated him. Emma never listened to suggestions Carlos had about the kids, rarely had them ready when he arrived to pick them up, and usually sent them to him with dirty clothes. Carlos had twin girls that he loved very much, but there was so much conflict between their mother and him that his time with his daughters was often sad.

Julia and the rest of the family often got on his case for "not standing up to Emma." This was hard on Carlos, who was doing everything he could think of to make things better. The pointed suggestions of Julia and other family members didn't help a bit. They only made him feel more down. He knew what his legal limitations were in dealing with Emma, but it seemed that his family always wanted him to do more.

Finally one day Carlos spoke up. He said, "Julia, I can't stand your advice anymore. It's getting to me bad. You and the rest of the family keep telling me what I should do about Emma, and I keep telling you I tried, and it doesn't work. I don't know what else to say to you. I feel like you hate me. To be honest with you, I am starting to get a little upset. I can only do so much, and that's all.

Maybe some day I'll be able to do what you think, but for now this is all I can do."

He told her plainly that he was doing everything he could, and he let her know how he felt about her constant comments. For the first time, Julia actually listened. As they talked further, she told him about her frustration of being powerless to help and admitted that she probably went overboard because of it.

This conversation didn't change how things went with Emma, but it did change how things were going with Julia and the rest of his family, and that made things easier by itself.

Think now of adults who have a big influence in your life. They may be the people in the circle that you drew earlier. Answer the following questions about each of them: Does he encourage you to stay involved with your child or tell you it isn't worth it? Does she help you see your child's mother objectively or does she cut her down? Does he listen patiently to you or tell you what to do? Does she encourage you to stay calm and play fair or tell you to "treat your ex as bad as she treats you"?

Stay closely connected with the people on your list who are supportive of you and your relationship with your kids, the ones that encourage you to stay involved, help you see things objectively, and encourage you to stay calm. If there are few people like that in your life, seek out understanding relatives, go to a counselor, or join a support group, and speak to them about what's going on with you.

Stepchildren and Other Children

As a live-away dad you may have more than just live-away kids in your life. You may have a new partner's children, kids you have with her, and your former partner's new biological and stepchildren. Although you don't raise all these children, you do have an important relationship with them, and they with each other.

Visualize all these active children sitting on one huge teeter-totter. Any shifting around by one child affects everybody else. Keeping that teeter-totter balanced is a real challenge. Meeting the needs of children—even if it's just your own—is a balancing act as well. The patience, compassion, and flexibility required to deal with all these children—yours, hers, ours, and theirs—can be challenging indeed.

Children need time to adjust to changing family relationships. The excitement of your union with a new partner is not automatically going to create harmony among all family members. Children each have their own personalities, histories, temperaments, loyalties, fears, moods, weak points, and strengths. Be very careful that you don't expect them to become instant friends with each other. Some children within an extended family may never become close friends.

Allow and encourage stepchildren to maintain close bonds with their father and other relatives. These are important relationships. Let them warm to you and other new people in their lives at their own pace, as long as that takes—and it could take years. The safer these kids feel with you (safety comes by being accepted for who they are) the more they will feel comfortable with you. Like healing your own wounds of the separation, it can't be rushed.

A common area of conflict I see between live-away dads and their new partners is in discipline of children. Both parents bring with them their own ways of parenting, and they often clash. He feels she's too lenient. She feels he's too strict. He thinks the kids don't show enough respect. She thinks he doesn't understand them. Both struggle with how to parent their own children and their partner's children in this new household.

One way some parents work out these differences is to allow the biological parent to be the main disciplinarian of their own children, with the other parent supplying backup as necessary. This provides for more consistent parenting for children. Work with your new partner on these parenting struggles, and do so away from the children.

One dad I had in individual counseling, Larry, was very upset about how his teenage stepchildren behaved. He considered them to be lazy and spoiled. Neither he nor their mother could get them to do chores around the house, get a job, or do their homework.

After years of trying to get their mother to stick to limits and demand cooperation around the house, Larry gave up. He stopped doing things with the kids. Actually he ignored them. They lived in the same house, but he stayed angry, and they avoided him. He gradually withdrew from their mom, and she teamed up more with her kids.

By the time Larry came to counseling, things were pretty bad. During counseling, things got better for a while. Larry tried listening to his wife's point of view. He tried not expecting so much. He tried being less demanding about the children's chores and homework. But none of it worked. Things began sliding back to their old patterns until Larry accepted the fact that he couldn't change his wife or her kids.

At that point Larry felt he had two choices. He could learn to live with the frustrations of the house while he looked at the positives he got from his marriage, or he could leave. He didn't want to leave, so he learned how to stay. He started to talk to his wife more and do things with her again. He loosened up with her children a bit, and when they got on his nerves he went to another room, got involved with something else, and let the kids be his wife's problem. He tried to do these things without anger and often succeeded. His goal was to let go of what he couldn't control and be as helpful as he could with the influence he had.

Things got better. The kids didn't change a heck of a lot (many young people do their growing up in their twenties), but Larry did. He accepted that there was nothing else he could do. He stopped being so angry and withdrawn because they didn't do things his way. Life in that home became easier to handle. Larry still got frustrated, but he recognized that there was nothing else he could do to change them or their mother, and when he did that he could relax more.

If your new partner's parenting techniques bother you, see if she will set aside specific times to talk with you in more depth about your concerns. Read books or articles about parenting and talk with each other about them. Discuss the things you like about her parenting, and try to do more of them yourself. Emphasize what works rather than what doesn't.

PART III

Navigating the Court System

The decisions made in family court have a powerful influence over our lives and the lives of our children. Because the legal system is so foreign to us and the stakes are so high, some dads become suspicious of not only the ability of legal professionals, but their intent as well. These dads react with hostility throughout the legal process. This can harm their chances of getting what they want.

Courts are often imperfect, but they are not out to get dads. In fact, they are often a powerful ally. The legal system can be instrumental in assuring that fathers maintain contact with their children when there is no other way for them to get it.

To give yourself the best chance for success in court, present yourself in an even-tempered manner. Show court personnel that you are a reasonable and caring father. Convince them with your actions that you work rationally toward meeting your child's needs.

CHAPTER 8

Parents Versus Courts

"All sides in a trial want to hide at least some of the truth."
—ALAN M. DERSHOWITZ

W hen parents agree on decisions about their children, courts have a limited role in their lives. It is only when parents can't agree together that the judicial system makes decisions for them. When this happens, both parents often leave court feeling unfairly treated and misunderstood. Depending upon the ability, time, resources, training of individuals in the system, and the laws governing that state, those parents might be right.

But legal systems never were very effective in resolving family conflict. More important, they don't have to be when parents work together. When parents work together they are in the driver's seat and the courts are in the backseat, which is where they belong and where they prefer to be. Parents frequently come to court with major disputes: clashes over paternity, division of property, time with the children, child support, conflicts about how the children are raised, and many other issues. They frequently leave court feeling cheated. It is no wonder that blame flies fast and furious.

But where should the blame land when parents are unhappy? I see only three options when looking for whom to blame. First, the judicial system is at fault. Second, the parents are to blame. Third, the parents and the system share the responsibility. Let's take a look at these three choices.

Choice One: It's the System's Fault

It's all the fault of the system, a hodgepodge of antiquated laws run by lazy and ignorant bureaucrats who don't care, a conspiracy for lawyers to make money. Officials don't take the time to know what is going on in the child's life and have their minds made up in advance. They don't investigate information given to them. They are easily suckered in by the other parent, and they don't listen to what the kids want. They either don't give any meaningful feedback about what they are doing with cases, or they make statements about what is going to happen and it doesn't.

Choice Two: It's the Parents' Fault

Outsiders may say the following about one or both parents: "They're all screwed up and completely selfish. If they really cared about their kids, they'd stop fighting with each other. They shouldn't have had kids in the first place."

When parents blame each other, dads may believe the following: She is totally selfish. The kids do anything they want, and she can't control them. She just wants them so she can get the child support. She acts like she owns the kids. When I drive over to get them for the weekend she changes plans at the last minute without telling me. The house is a mess, and she doesn't take care of the kids right. She's trying to turn them against me. When I bring our children back to her house she interrogates them to see what we did. She has a new boyfriend and tells the kids to call him "daddy."

Moms may believe this: He always has his relatives watching the kids. He's too rough with the children when he does have them. He only cares about himself and is just mad because he has to pay child support. He never played with the kids when we were together and now he acts like "superdad." He has the fun times, but I have to do all the shopping, cooking, cleaning, and saying "no." After finally telling the kids he'll pick them up for the weekend he comes over late or not at all. He lies to the kids about me. He doesn't come to see our children; he comes to check up on me. He has a girlfriend now and tells the kids they have a new mom.

Choice Three: Parents and the System Share the Responsibility

Now let's look at the third choice. Parents and court systems both contribute to the problem. My experience working in the system as a social worker, as well as being subjected to it as a father, tells me that this is most accurate. I don't think that everything can be blamed only on the parents or only on the courts. The responsibility is shared. There are imperfect parents and imperfect courts.

The legal system is very rigid, and it does not effectively resolve personal conflicts. It is often ineffective in enforcing laws, and some of the laws it is entrusted to carry out are unfair. Another problem for courts is that small mistakes parents make may be too minor to warrant judicial involvement, and big ones may be so serious that no amount of court intervention can solve them.

All parents also make mistakes with their kids, and if parents were more effective in solving their own problems, the courts wouldn't be involved much at all. Obviously, some parents make bigger mistakes than others, and these must be responded to, but it is not only the parents or only the system that is responsible for making mistakes or repairing them. That's why we are better off in the long run working on our own emotional growth as much as possible. Regardless of the challenges put before us, the way that we conduct ourselves around our children and their mother—or in the courtroom—has a powerful influence over how well our lives go.

Should I Take Her Back to Court?

There are a limitless number of child-rearing actions and decisions that separated parents can—and do—fight about. Are the kids fed right? Are they properly supervised? Should they be disciplined more or less strictly? Is child support paid? Is the amount fair? Is it spent on the kids? Do the kids have too much freedom? Are they spoiled? Should they have the car so often? Do they have a curfew? Is the curfew appropriate? Is it enforced? Should the child attend summer school, play an instrument, go to my church, be allowed certain friends? The questions go on and on.

You want to be a loving dad who supports and protects his children. But how do you do that when they don't live with you and you disagree with what their mother does? How do you sort out your concerns about fathering? One thing that helps is to ask and answer the following question for yourself in every difficult situation that comes up. That question is "What is in my child's best interests?"

That is the inquiry that guides all interventions by social service and legal authorities. It's also the question they expect you to ask for yourself. They are listening for the answer in your words—and more important—looking for it in your actions. But it's not a simple question. Emotions may get in the way of answering it well, and as great as emotions are—they connect us to other people and give life it's fullness—they can also cloud our judgment.

So be aware of your emotions and recognize that although you can't control them absolutely, you can understand them, channel them, and turn them into one of your greatest strengths. As you do so you will develop a greater ability to meet your children's needs.

As a court-appointed social worker I've been involved in many court disputes between angry parents. Some of those parents left court feeling they had lost, and some felt they had won. Within weeks, however, even the winners often felt cheated and misunderstood. The court order was not followed exactly. Things did not go as planned. The arguments resumed.

By setting rules parents must abide by, courts serve a vital role in protecting children from harm. Unfortunately, in the heat of battle, many parents see harm to their children as greater than it is. Without realizing it, they use the courts to act out their frustration rather than to protect their children.

What are you to do when court intervention seems insufficient? Is going to court and battling over issues—or returning to court and battling again over the same issues—in your child's best interests? When does the arguing between parents do more harm than good? Is there a point at which it is best to stop fighting and acknowledge that there are things neither you nor the courts can change about your child's mother? The following examples about improper clothes and Christmas cards will help answer these questions.

Improper clothes

Every time your daughter comes to your home for the weekend she does not have the proper clothes. You've spoken to her mother several times about it, but nothing changes. What should you do?

Stop a minute and look at this question as objectively as possible. First of all, what exactly does "proper" mean? Who decides what is proper and improper? Are wrinkled clothes improper? Dirty clothes? How dirty? Torn clothes? How torn? Clothes that fit badly? How badly? Clothes that are improper for a special occasion? Clothes that are not warm enough for weather conditions? No change of clothes at all?

If you believe that your children are without the "proper" clothing, does it help them when you hold a grudge and argue with their mother? No. Is it helpful to take some action? Yes, but what action you take is what matters.

Let's take the worst-case scenario. Let's say your children's mother sends the kids to you with torn, dirty, poorly fitted, inappropriate clothes, or no change of clothes at all. She does it every time you have them, and she does it solely to get back at you! What do you do? You have several options.

Talk it over with her

You could talk with her about it. Let her know your reasons for wanting the kids to have the proper clothes. Tell her how frustrated you get when they don't have the right clothes. This may get her to listen, or it may have no effect at all, but it's still important to at least let her know what you want.

Take it to court

You could take it to court. It's unlikely that courts would address this relatively minor issue, but let's say they do, and the best happens—a ruling is issued in your favor that spells out in detail what she must do in the future about clothing. But what if she doesn't obey the order or obeys it halfway and works around the edges of compliance? The time, money, and emotional energy required to verify and enforce court orders can be astounding, so what do you do? Go back to court again? It would be great if court rulings were carried out exactly, but in reality they often aren't.

Argue with her or withdraw

With or without court intervention you can argue with your children's mom. You can lose your temper with the kids. At the other extreme, you can back away from your kids and see them less and less. I've seen dads respond both ways out of frustration when they didn't know what else to do. There is another choice.

Be committed to making it work

You could look at yourself, acknowledge your frustration and hurt, and find solutions that require nothing from her. What are some possible solutions you could come up with on your own?

You could clean your children's clothes. You could mend them yourself. You could replace them with other clothes or buy better fitting ones. If you cannot afford new clothes, you could buy more from resale shops or rummage sales. If your children take your clothes to their mother's house and they come back to you in poor condition or don't come back at all, you could stop sending them with the kids and keep those clothes at your place. That way you would always have something adequate.

Are these solutions ideal? No. Far from it. Is it fair that anyone should have to resort to them? No. And there are many reasons why it's not fair. Kids shouldn't have to have two sets of clothing. One is enough. It should be no big hassle for her to send the kids to you with decent clothes. Your child support already pays for clothes. It's a total waste to buy extra clothes when they outgrow them so quickly. It would be more efficient for one parent to do the shopping rather than both parents.

This unfairness may be a source of tremendous frustration for you, but as tough as it is, recognize that if you focus on fairness, you sidetrack yourself. You get trapped in looking at what's fair rather than what makes things better.

The question that most helps your children remains the same through all this. It is not "What is fair?" It is "What is in my child's best interests?" If you have made a decision to stay in your children's lives no matter what, put their best interests ahead of fairness. Putting their needs first requires you to do many things that seem unfair to you in order to find solutions that work. The more you make these adjustments in yourself, the better your relationship with your kids will get, because you'll be growing. Struggles will continue, but solutions will begin to appear within them.

Christmas cards

Jeff had two children aged eight and twelve. They lived with their mother, Amy. Jeff and Amy were never married, but they had lived together for ten years. He loved their children very much and felt a great loss when Amy and he broke up.

Amy and Jeff got along reasonably well after breaking up, but one thing that really bothered Jeff was that his kids didn't send Christmas cards to his mother. His mom sent her grandchildren cards and a little money every birthday and Christmas, and she was hurt that they didn't seem to appreciate what she, or Jeff, did for them.

The first Christmas after Amy and Jeff separated, the kids gave Grandma a nice little gift that she really liked. They didn't give her anything the next Christmas. Jeff tried to keep his cool. He talked to Amy numerous times about having the kids show more appreciation. He told her he didn't need them to spend any money on Grandma; he just wanted them to make her something or send a card. Next Christmas came and went with nothing for Grandma.

Jeff wondered why Amy got them to give gifts once but not again. It seemed like such a simple thing, and it would make their grandmother so happy. When he tried to talk with Amy about it, she said she was too busy to get the kids to send anything or that the kids just didn't want to. Jeff's anger silently grew within him until, one Christmas Day, he got into a screaming match with Amy. The kids saw the whole thing. Christmas was ruined. Jeff felt terrible.

Could this have been avoided? Yes. Jeff could have helped his kids make and send the cards himself. He was angry that Amy didn't take care of things, but he missed the opportunity to do so himself. It wouldn't have been exactly the same if he had done it with the kids instead of Amy, but they would still learn the values he wanted them to, and his mom would get the cards. While this isn't a perfect solution, or maybe even a fair one, it works, and it keeps the kids out of the middle.

Except for the blowup, this situation might seem minor, but it's not. It certainly doesn't warrant court involvement, but conflicts between separated parents are often like this. Such incidents may appear trivial, but each interaction with your child's mother is important, and besides, if you succeed with minor conflicts, you gain practice at finding solutions for larger ones. You also create an atmosphere of cooperation in which all problems are more likely to be worked out.

Actually, little arguments are often more than they appear. Many are expressions of unresolved feelings and power struggles lying below the surface. Feelings so strong that parents have difficulty expressing them directly—or even recognizing them. As a result, they come out indirectly in battles over minor things.

Many times we dads have strong opinions about how our former wife or lover should do things. Sometimes we're correct, and sometimes we aren't. Unfortunately, things often don't go the way we want regardless of whether we are correct or not. So in some ways, right and wrong doesn't really matter. What does matter is that we do our best to make things better.

All separated parents have their own unique sets of parenting problems, joys, and responsibilities. You may never understand or appreciate hers, and she may never understand or appreciate yours. But most moms care tremendously about their children and do a good job parenting them, and most dads care tremendously about their children and do a good job parenting them.

Don't confuse the conflict between your children's mother and you with the totally different skill of parenting. Both of you may be a lot better at raising your children than at getting along with each other, so be sure your judgment of how well she handles the kids is not contaminated by your anger at how she deals with you. Don't try to outparent her either. Sometimes, all you can do is parent your kids to the best of your ability when you are with them, regardless of how she does things.

Strange as it sounds, we empower our children and ourselves when we do things we shouldn't have to do—especially if we do them without blaming the other parent. It may not be fair, but this is not about fairness. It's not about getting even. It is about doing what works for our kids and ourselves.

Only involve courts when the issue is very important, and be realistic about what you are likely to get from your efforts. Your power to get what you want with your children results primarily from your ability to evaluate situations realistically, make changes in your own behavior, and work things out with your children's mother whether the courts are involved or not.

The courts aren't bad any more than you or your child's mother is bad. All courts and parents are imperfect though, so think of the courts and your child's mother as imperfect rather than intentionally bad.

I know of situations in which courts have rendered terrible decisions. In some, the parents had every reason to believe, based upon the comments and actions of court personnel, that their case was looking very good, only to find out in the final court hearing that everything was reversed. Decisions were made that went completely against what they had expected. Decisions that, frankly, made no sense, and although this does not happen frequently, one time is too often.

Even parents who don't go through such dramatic changes know the agony of things going badly in court—and of not being with their children. It's almost impossible to know how painful those circumstances can be for live-away dads and live-away moms. In fact, you have to be one to fully understand it. I hope the reader realizes that some people truly understand what you are going through. We who have been there say to you, "Don't give up. Your children need you. Stay involved and rewards will come to your children and you in ways you cannot yet understand."

CHAPTER 9

Insider's Report: What I Looked for as a Family Court Social Worker

"Justice cannot be for one side only, but must be for both . . ."
—ELEANOR ROOSEVELT

I n this chapter I give you an insider's view of what I looked for during the five years in which it was my job as a social worker to conduct custody studies and parenting-time (visitation) mediation for a county court. Your job when dealing with professionals, whether they be social workers, judges, attorneys, therapists, police, or any others, is to conduct yourself in such a way that they will have confidence that you are a capable and caring parent.

A wealthy businessman once told me there are three things that are mandatory for success in business: location, location, and location. Applying that thought here, I suggest to you that the three most important things you can do when dealing with court and social service personnel are to express yourself calmly, express yourself calmly, and express yourself calmly.

When I say "express yourself," I mean tell professionals what is on your mind. Don't sit back and say nothing. Develop the confidence and conviction to say what is important to you. "Calmly" refers to how you say what's on your mind. If you become angry or run your children's mother down in front of professionals, it will not convince them that you are a rational and objective parent who can put his strong personal feelings aside to meet the emotional needs of his children.

If you have concerns about how your children's mom is parenting, or you believe that her actions directly harm your children, say so, but say it without blowing up. Remember, you can only say what's on you mind. You can't make others believe you. Professionals will be affected by what you say *and* how you say it. If they see outbursts of anger from you inside the office, they may wonder if you can control yourself outside it.

A key to dealing with professionals is to focus on strengths rather than weaknesses. Let them know what you do well with your children, why you want to be more involved in their lives, and how your involvement will help them as children and adults.

Because there is variation in the ways custody studies and parenting-time mediation is carried out from professional to professional and state to state, what I thought about and did with cases might be different from what happens in yours. Still, I think the information in this chapter will give you a good idea of what other social workers might be thinking, and how they might react, when conducting custody studies or parenting-time mediation.

Custody Studies

When parents cannot decide between themselves where their child will live after a separation, either or both parents can ask the court to grant them custody. Disputes over custody and placement of children usually involve a judge, attorneys for parents, a guardian ad litem (an individual, usually an attorney, appointed by the court to represent the children's interests), and a social worker. A psychologist may conduct psychological evaluations of both parents and, possibly, the children.

As a court-appointed social worker for the family court, my role, and the role of other social workers whom I worked with was to investigate the circumstances of each parent's life, evaluate how those circumstances would affect their children, and recommend a course of action to the judge.

We obtained information for our evaluations from several sources. We spoke with each parent separately in their homes once, met one or two additional times with each in our offices, and conducted one interview session with both parents together. If the children were school age, we interviewed their teachers and gathered other school information such as grades, attendance, and behavior with other children.

We asked each parent to respond in writing to several questions about their parenting and obtained references regarding their parenting ability. Police reports, psychological evaluations, or other relevant sources of information were reviewed as well.

The home visit

Home visits gave me an opportunity to see the environment children lived in or might live in. I was not concerned about how expensive the home was. I wanted to see how safe it was, if it was reasonably clean, where the children would sleep, and how much the home reflected thought by that parent about his or her children's physical and psychological needs. When possible, I arranged appointments when the kids would be there so that I could observe how the parent interacted with them in a familiar environment.

When interviewing parents at home, I asked them about how they disciplined their kids, how they communicated with them, and what they could tell me about their children's interests, activities, and personalities. Also significant was how each parent spent time with his or her children, how he or she supported them in school, and what each considered to be his or her strengths and weaknesses as a parent. I tried to assess if the parent's approach with the child was positive or negative, controlling or flexible, open or defensive, nurturing or punishing, attentive or uninvolved.

I wanted to know about each parent's work and residence histories. If an individual had several job changes or changes in living arrangements or locations in a short span of time, I wanted to know why. I felt that frequent moves were a possible sign of instability on the parent's part and a potential problem for the child who would have to adjust to them if the moves continued. I asked each parent how they felt about the other parent's involvement with the children, and how they handled conflicts that came up.

I tried to evaluate whether parents struck a realistic balance between their children's needs and their own. Some parents gave too little to their children. They seemed too busy with work, friends, or their new partners to spend quality time with their children. Some parents seemed to focus too much on their kids. They lived for their children in such a sacrificing way that they didn't maintain a healthy balance in their life.

I was impressed with parents who could keep parenting in perspective, who could balance their children's needs with their own— parents who recognized that their children come first but that they could not be helpful to their children if they neglected themselves. I looked for parents who could nurture their children but also allow them to separate from them as is the task, ultimately, of all children.

Joint interviews

In addition to separate interviews with parents, I always carried out one interview session with both parents together. For parents, that meeting was the most difficult part of the custody study. Most did not want to be in the same room with their former partners, and the tension was high. But that meeting was necessary. It helped me understand the conflicts between parents and how they treated each other.

Joint-interview sessions gave moms and dads an opportunity to hear exactly what the other parent was saying about the custody dispute and each other's parenting. Parents could then respond directly to those statements. In these sessions I got a better idea of what parents thought about discipline, communication, school, house rules, and each other. I got a sense of how reasonable each parent was, and I learned not just what parents disagreed about but how they disagreed.

Talking with children

When conducting custody studies I always met the children. I tried to talk to them both with a parent present and alone. When possible, I spoke with them in each home. When meeting with children, I tried to be gentle and respectful with my questions. I didn't want to stir up painful emotions, and I didn't want them to think that telling me how they felt meant they were siding with one parent or the other.

Generally, the older the child, the more detailed my questions were. I did not ask young children who they wanted to live with or which parent treated them best. Instead, I observed their play. I tried to see how happy and relaxed they were, watched how they interacted with their parents, and looked at how their parents dealt with them.

With children aged seven to fourteen or so, I still avoided direct questions about who they wanted to live with, because I didn't want to give them the impression that they could decide that issue. I did ask more specific questions about things such as what they liked to do with their friends, how school was going, what they did with each parent, what discipline their parents used with them, and what they liked about each house.

I was more direct with my questions to teenagers, especially the older or more sophisticated ones. Those interviews included questions about how they got along with each parent, what it was like at each parent's home, and what types of rules and consequences they had in each residence. I also asked some teenagers which parent they wanted to live with and why.

Although there is no specific legal age at which courts must allow minors to decide where they will live, some courts begin to take into account the wishes of children around the ages of twelve to fourteen and older. Many times, parents agreed on where their older teens would live and the custody dispute was only over the younger children. I got more specific in my questions with teenagers whose placement had not been decided, but I always made it clear to them that their parents or the judge would make the final decision.

Some parents wanted their children to choose who they would live with. These were usually the parents who thought their child would pick them. I let those parents know that, except for some teenagers, I would not ask their children who they wanted to live with and that living arrangements would not be their children's choice. I did my best to make it clear to these parents that putting young children in the position of making such decisions is unfair to them, because they are not responsible for their parents' separation and should not be required, allowed, or manipulated into choosing one parent over another.

Talking with teachers

I always talked to children's teachers, because I considered school personnel to be a valuable source of independent information. Those interviews sometimes gave me insight into the quality of parental involvement in the school, and I could see if there were any unusually positive or negative reactions a child might have to either parent.

I also inquired about the children's school grades, attendance, behavior, and peer relationships. I wasn't looking for straight A's or perfect attendance. I was interested in seeing if they attended school regularly, got along reasonably well with other children, seemed happy, and got passing grades.

References, written responses, and reports

I asked parents to respond in writing to a variety of questions, including their reasons for wanting their children to live with them, what they felt they offered their children as a parent, and why their children should be placed in their home. I asked parents for names and addresses of nonrelatives who could serve as references about their parenting and then sent those people a brief questionnaire about the referring parent's activities, discipline techniques, and interactions with the children. I understood that parents would put their best foot forward in written questions and use references that would speak well of them, but that additional information remained a valuable piece of the whole picture I was trying to see.

I reviewed police reports, psychological evaluations, or other reports by professionals that could give clues to a parent's mental stability and life choices. Psychological evaluations done specifically for the custody dispute were helpful, but it was not common for police reports and other professional reports to contain enough additional information to have a strong impact on cases.

When you deal with social workers, realize that they do not expect you to be a child psychiatrist, but they do need to know that you have a thorough understanding of your children's physical and emotional needs, activities, interests, and personalities. You don't have to be a great speaker or thinker, you just need to express your thoughts in plain and honest terms. You need not be perfect, but you need to lead your life successfully enough to meet your children's physical and emotional needs.

Parenting-Time (Visitation) Mediation

In custody disputes, physical placement of the children is contested. The main question there is "Which home is the best one for the children to live in?" In parenting-time mediation, physical placement of the children has already been determined. Here, the main question is "What arrangements can be made that result in children having meaningful contact with both their parents?"

Parenting-time mediation deals with many types of conflict. These topics could include arguing between parents, problems with last minute schedule changes, the amount and scheduling of the live-away dad's time with his children, denial of father's time with his kids, young children being given the choice of whether they want to go with the father, parents not having the children prepared to go at exchange time, parents not being at the pick-up or drop-off point at the agreed upon time, and disputes over when or where the children are to be exchanged.

Court-ordered mediation is an important tool for working out parenting disputes, and it is available in many states. It is usually started by a dad who is upset about inadequate access to his child and may be initiated by either parent months or years after physical placement of the children have been determined.

I recommend mediation to fathers and mothers who experience ongoing conflict over parenting time or other important matters that they have not been able to resolve on their own. It often does not require an attorney, can usually be completed in a few months, and, in many states, the conclusions reached in mediation become legally binding.

Parents in mediation that I conducted frequently believed strongly that the other parent's lifestyle hurt their children and that I could require the other parent to change. But I couldn't, and it was difficult for them to accept that the way in which the other parent conducted his or her life was not a factor in mediation unless it directly and seriously affected the child.

I conducted my mediations with the core belief that two parents are better than one, and that philosophy was shared by all court and social-service professionals I knew. Our job was to help parents come up with arrangements that allowed both of them meaningful time with their children without interference by the other parent. This was often difficult, however, because parents saw their actions as protection, but those actions often looked like interference to me. My job was to tell the difference between protection and interference, safeguard each parent's right to parent, and help them reach agreement.

The mediation process

Although parenting-time mediation is extremely important, it has less impact on family members and requires less information than custody disputes. Therefore, social workers conducting parenting-time mediation in the county I worked in usually did not seek school input, obtain references, give parents written question-naires, interview children, review outside reports, or go to parents' homes. We wanted to keep children out of the middle as much as possible and keep parents focused on resolving their problems to-gether.

When conducting parenting-time mediation, I had one inter-view session with each parent separately, followed by two to four joint sessions. Experience taught me that if things could not be re-solved in three or four joint sessions, twenty would have gotten us no further. In individual interviews I learned what each parent's complaints were about the schedule, the other parent, or anything else he or she wanted to talk about. In the joint sessions we ad-dressed those issues and tried to resolve them.

I learned very quickly in my mediation career to keep my opin-ions about a case to myself until very near the end of the process. I know that was frustrating for parents who were anxious to find out what I was thinking as we went along, but it was the only way I could be fair to them because my opinion changed so much in the course of the meetings.

It was common for me to walk away from my first individual interview, whether it was with the mom or the dad, thinking that the other one was a real monster. From the first parent I spoke with alone, I usually heard detailed stories of the uncaring, harm-ful, selfish things the other parent did. I felt like stringing that par-ent up in the nearest tree. Then I interviewed the second parent. There I heard equally convincing stories of the first parent's harm-ful behavior. By the time I left that interview I was ready to march back to the first parent and string *that* one up.

Both parents usually had totally opposite views of events that occurred between them—but neither parent was lying. Both of them believed what they said, but they seemed to have had two completely different experiences. That's why I had to be so careful not to accept either parent's version as *the truth*. There were *two truths*, and I needed time to sort them out.

The value of joint interviews was that parents had to be more careful about what they said because exaggerations and partial stories could be confronted by the other parent. Both adults had to speak more objectively.

My goal in parenting-time mediation was to assist parents in reaching a compromise they could both accept. If we accomplished that, and we usually did, I would then mail a letter to both of them specifying those points, have them review it for accuracy, and sign and return it to me. I would then submit that letter to the judge, and it would became the basis of a court order.

If parents could not reach consensus, I told them exactly what I was going to recommend to the judge on each issue they couldn't resolve. If they still did not reach agreement, I sent a report to the judge detailing the issues that had been agreed upon and made recommendations on what to do with those that had not. It was then up to the judge to determine the details of the final agreement.

Evaluating Parenting Abilities

In parenting-time mediation I did not have to determine who was the "best" parent. I simply had to determine that both met a minimal standard of mental health and stability of lifestyle. Almost all parents did that, so the goal of mediation was to set up a parenting-time schedule that was fair to both parents while assuring that live-away parents had meaningful access to their children.

Parents frequently felt that the other parent was doing things outside the mediation sessions that were harmful to their children. Mom often felt that dad's anger or lack of follow-through was harming the kids, and dad often felt that mom was intentionally manipulating the kids against him or sabotaging their time. It was common for mothers and fathers to be afraid that I didn't see those harmful parental behaviors.

I believe I did see most of this parental behavior clearly, but that behavior didn't have as much impact on me as parents wanted or feared. As much as I may have disagreed with some of that behavior, it was seldom harmful enough to significantly affect each parent's right to contact with his or her children.

As I worked with parents to come up with reasonable parenting-time schedules, there were four things I paid attention to: emotional stability, parenting skills, alcohol or other drug abuse, and support of the other parent's time with the children. There were two sources of information about these points: what happened outside my office and my own observations of both parents.

Information about what happened outside the office came from two sources. One included independent information such as police reports, psychological evaluations, and mental health histories, but, as I said earlier, I seldom used that type of information because the mediation process did not call for such in-depth investigations. The second source of information about what happened outside the office was the parents' reports of it, but each parent often presented very different views of what had occurred.

Because of these limitations, the most relevant information I had about parents was usually what I observed or learned in my office. In the office I saw for myself how parents conducted themselves and got the best understanding I could of incidents outside the office. Unfortunately, some dads seemed to feel outgunned in mediation. They thought that women are better talkers, but I didn't necessarily find that they were. I consider some women to be more frequent talkers and more comfortable in verbal communication, but that doesn't necessarily make them better communicators or better parents.

Some mothers sounded better in sessions because they talked a bit more about their children's personalities and interests. I was always aware, however, that it's easier for live-in parents to talk about the details of their children's lives because they observe those events daily, and I took that into account when assessing each parent's knowledge of his or her kids.

But being a live-away dad does not diminish your ability to get to know your kids better in the time you have together, even in cases where it is done primarily by phone or letter. Use all methods available to you to get closer to your kids and to share your knowledge of them with the mediator. Mediators do want to know, so express your thoughts about your kids. You don't have to talk like your children's mom. Do it your way. You don't have to say things "right." You simply want to give the mediator confidence that you know and understand your children.

Emotional stability

Of the four things I evaluated in parenting time, emotional stability of parents was probably the most important. Parents in mediation are often angry and afraid, and I accepted that strong emotions would be expressed there. A primary objective of mine was to see whether parents were healthy enough to function well in spite of strong emotions, and most were. To a certain extent, I saw angry or manipulative reactions as normal. Not necessarily healthy, but "normal" in the sense that they were the norm, and not necessarily desirable, but understandable—and we were usually able to work through strong emotions well enough to come up with a workable parenting-time compromise.

Although I accepted that feelings ran high in mediation sessions, I did not accept verbal abuse or physical threats by parents, and any time such behavior occurred I let parents know I would end the session if it continued. I informed them that extreme stubbornness or excessive venting of emotions in sessions could decrease their ability to get what they wanted from mediation, because it would cause me to doubt their ability to stay calm away from my office.

Many parents expressed strong anger and upset in sessions, and although that is understandable, emotions that are so strong that they constantly interfere with mediation cause the mediator to think that your anger will spill over onto your children. Deal with your frustration in other ways outside the mediator's office, use the communication techniques I've discussed in this book when in mediation, and show the mediator that you can deal constructively with your children's mother in spite of your anger, fear, or sadness.

Parenting skills

Because parents were usually in mediation to iron out problems with the quantity or circumstances of each parent's time with his or her children, not parenting skills, I did not spend a lot of time asking about parenting techniques unless one of the parents brought it up. If it was not an issue to them, we could avoid it in sessions.

When parenting actions were brought up, I asked more questions about them, such as who was responsible for watching the children when the parent was not there, what the parent did with the kids, what discipline techniques they used, and other relevant questions. When I concluded that the parenting behaviors in question were not a serious problem, I tried to help the concerned parent accept that the other one parented differently than he or she did but that is not the same as parenting wrong.

If I became concerned, from all the information available to me, that a certain parenting behavior might be harmful, I pointed it out to the parent doing it and encouraged him or her to change that behavior. If the parent did not work on change, I had three choices. I could let it go if it wasn't serious enough to pursue further, I could recommend that the court require parenting restrictions that I considered appropriate, or I could refer the matter to a protective-service worker for investigation.

Alcohol or other drug use

When allegations of substance abuse were made by parents I did my best to get to the bottom of them. Accusations against parents were difficult to prove, however, and corrective actions were hard to enforce. It was particularly difficult to place restrictions on live-in parents, because they were responsible for their children's daily care. If a live-away parent violated court-ordered rules, access to his or her children could more realistically be restricted.

Because it is so difficult to restrict live-in parents' time or conduct with their children, parenting-time mediation is probably not the best place for live-away dads to pursue their concerns of alcohol or drug problems by their children's mothers. Those allegations might best be dealt with as part of a protective-service investigation or custody dispute.

When allegations of alcohol or other drug abuse against live-away parents were brought up, I would take no action if I felt those accusations were groundless. If I thought substance abuse might be affecting children, I recommended restrictions on the live-away parent's conduct. The most common restriction was that the live-away parent not use any alcohol or drugs during, and twenty-four hours prior to, his or her time with the children.

Live-in moms often considered this sanction too mild and live-away dads felt it was too severe. Eventually, however, both usually accepted this restriction as a compromise, and it became part of the judge's order. It helped mothers feel better about their children going to their fathers' homes. The dads usually denied the abuse and resented restrictions as an invasion of their privacy but stated that because they did not abuse substances, they would accept the restrictions as a necessary compromise.

Support of the other parent's time with the children

I did my best to evaluate whether moms or dads interfered with the time or activities of the other parent. Because live-in moms are with their children the most, I was particularly interested in finding out how supportive they were about the dads' time. I considered it my job to see that both parents had a meaningful role in the lives of their children, and I did what I could in this difficult situation to assure that that happened.

I spent a lot of time trying to get resistant moms to see why their children's fathers are important to their children. I worked hard to develop a parenting-time schedule that gave dads meaning-ful time with their kids. I let live-in parents know that if I believed they were not cooperative in allowing the fathers that time, I would do my best to see that it was built into the schedule.

Loving Your Kids or Venting Your Frustration?

Dads enter custody studies and parenting-time mediation with great love for their children. Many also come with great anger at their children's mother and the court system. Some of this anger, I believe, is justified. It's almost impossible to avoid anger when faced with conflict with your children's mother, decreased contact with your own children, and increased financial obligations in the form of child support.

Whether you take your concerns to court or not, continue to look honestly at your own behavior. Be sure that you use the legal system to seek fairness for yourself and your children—not to vent your anger. Do your best to avoid losing your temper out of court as well. Do your kids hear arguments between you and their mother? Do they ever hear you complaining about her? Do you lose your patience with them, even a little bit, because you're angry at their mother? Do you lose your temper with your kids because they don't behave the way they would if they lived with you? If you answered "yes" to any of these questions, dedicate yourself to changing your behavior so that in the future you can answer "no" to them all.

Learn to deal with strong feelings effectively so that your chil-dren experience more of your love and less of your anger. It's un-derstandable that your frustration level is high, but your goal with your children and those around them is to have your love shine brighter.

CHAPTER 10

How to Succeed in Parenting-Time (Visitation) Mediation

"Success is more a function of consistent common sense than it is of genius."
—AN WANG

I f disagreements over time or activities with your children have become a source of conflict between you and your children's mother, voluntary or court-ordered mediation can help. This process can be valuable whether you are recently separated from your children or have been away for years.

In the county for which I conducted custody studies and parenting-time mediation, voluntary mediation occurred when both parents agreed to work together in setting new conditions on time or activities with their children. Court-ordered mediation required both parents to participate. It resulted in rules backed by the court, so both parents had to cooperate if they wanted to have an influence in the changes that would be made. Voluntary mediation can be helpful, but court-ordered mediation may be necessary if your child's mom will not agree to enter mediation or if you need the power of a court order to back decisions that are reached.

This chapter begins by examining whether time with children should be flexible or fixed. Then there is a look at strategies for successful negotiation of the three main aspects of parenting time: the ongoing schedule, holidays, and extended time periods. The chapter closes with twelve tips for success in parenting-time mediation.

Flexible Schedule Versus Fixed Schedule

Both flexible and fixed schedules typically provide live-away dads time with their children every other weekend, parts of holidays (often with more substantial time on Christmas and Easter), and approximately two to three weeks each summer.

With flexible schedules, live-away dads usually also have what is called "reasonable visitation," which is often interpreted by the courts to mean that he is able to see his children any time he gives twenty-four hours' notice to his children's mom provided it also works out for her.

A fixed schedule specifically details each parent's time with his or her child, including which specific days each parent has with the child and the exact time the contact starts and ends. There is no provision for "reasonable visitation," and exceptions are not encouraged.

I much prefer flexible schedules over fixed schedules when parents get along reasonably well, but when they don't, I believe fixed schedules are best. Recommending fixed schedules may seem strange coming from a live-away dad who believes in fathers getting meaningful time with their children, but I have found over the years that flexible schedules simply don't work in cases where there is great conflict and mistrust between parents.

One of the most frustrating things dads face in being separated from their children is the feeling that their children's mothers can control them through their kids. That feeling is understandable because the live-in parent does have more control over the children's schedules. As a result, when conflicts occur about when dad will be with the kids, the live-in parent usually has the last word.

Fixed schedules equalize that power imbalance. When fixed schedules are established, the live-away dad's time with his kids is completely his. He has as much right to his specific, predetermined time with his children as the live-in mom has to her time.

More important, with fixed schedules you no longer have to go through the degrading process of asking for time with your own children. You simply confirm your previously determined time. Sentences change from questions: "Joan, can I have the kids on Friday?" to statements: "Joan, I'll be there Friday at five P.M. See you then."

While I'm talking about words to use when arranging pick-up of the kids, I'll suggest some for dads who do have flexible schedules. Here too you start your communication about the pick-up time in the form of a statement rather than a question. This makes you feel less like you are asking for a favor, and conversations become a lot easier.

Instead of asking: "Joan, *can I get* Jenny next Friday for my brother's birthday party?" you make the statement: "Joan, *I'd like to have* Jenny next Friday for my brother's birthday party." You state your desire respectfully, of course, but the subtle difference is that you are no longer asking permission—you are stating what you want. You will need to communicate about the details just as you would if you'd started with a question, but you'll feel more comfortable in that conversation.

I recommend that fixed schedules be stuck to exactly, at least for the first couple years or so after they are established. No exceptions. It's important to stick to fixed schedules exactly because as soon as one parent asks for an exception, limits become fuzzy. A favor given has the price tag of a favor returned. Parents start to weigh out the relative value of exceptions and then ask for "equal" sacrifice by the other parent. Unfortunately, parents often can't agree on what's equal, or be patient if that favor isn't returned the way they think is fair, and arguments erupt.

Does a two hour early return time mean I get two extra hours next week for sure? If I ask to trade weekends with the kids, and this is more inconvenient for you and your family, how do we equalize that greater inconvenience? Do I have to give in more than you do? If I say "no" to one of your requests, are you going to get back at me by saying "no" to one of mine?

Fixed schedules and flexible schedules also impose different degrees of responsibility upon parents. An example might be a dad needing to work or fulfill another commitment when the children are scheduled to be with him, and they have to be taken to a friend's birthday party.

With a fixed schedule, dad has the full opportunity or problem (depending upon how you view it) of making arrangements to get the children to that event without giving that responsibility over to his children's mother. A flexible schedule, on the other hand, would allow him to more easily work out an arrangement with their mother in which she takes them to the event for him, or she keeps them that day and takes them from her house.

A disadvantage to flexible scheduling is that one or both parents might try to abuse it. In this example, the mom might argue against sending the kids with their dad at all that day, saying they would be with him so little that she should keep them and take them to the event herself. On the other hand, a dad might insist that the mom take the kids that day rather than him, just to hassle her or take the responsibility off his shoulders.

Neither of these reasons is fair to the other parent or the kids. It isn't fair to a dad who has a right to be responsible for all aspects of raising his children when they are with him. On the other hand, that mom has a right to make plans and enjoy her time away from the children. She should not have to worry that she's going to be required to make arrangements for their kids at the last minute.

With fixed schedules, dad's time with his children is totally his. Mom can say no more about how and when they spend it with him than he can say about how and when it's spent with her. This creates predictability for children in uncertain times and reduces some of the power imbalance that creates so much frustration in live-away dads.

Three Aspects of the Parenting-Time Schedule

In mediating parenting-time I learned that time with children could be separated into three main categories: the ongoing schedule, holidays, and extended time periods. Sometimes there are other areas of disagreement to be addressed, such as supervision of the children, religious upbringing, division of property, schooling, and others, too many to realistically address here. For those issues, the Dozen Keys to Successful Mediation described later in this chapter might be helpful, because they apply to scheduling conflicts and nonscheduling conflicts alike.

The ongoing schedule

The term "ongoing schedule" refers to the regular cycle of time that each parent has with his or her children throughout the year. As mentioned earlier, a typical schedule is for live-away parents to have the children with them every other weekend and possibly an additional weeknight evening each week. Some ongoing schedules might include more or less time depending upon things such as physical distance between parents, the ability of parents to cooperate with each other, work schedules, state laws, and established customs within different courts.

It's important to know what a typical ongoing schedule is in your area, because court and social-service personnel are reluctant to vary significantly from it unless the parents are in agreement. Demands far beyond the norm often result in expensive and fruitless court battles that only affect children and parents in negative ways. If, however, you request more time than is usually given, and you know you are not doing so to vent your anger, go for it. You may be able to get more time than the norm.

When I was a family-court mediator I often saw both parents enter mediation asking for more time than was realistic. Many times they did it because they didn't know what a typical ongoing schedule was, and other times they did so as a bargaining tactic.

What was difficult was dealing with parents who refused to change their positions. They'd come in with demands that were far beyond the norm and refuse to budge. A live-in mom, for example, would demand that the dad only have the kids one day every other weekend, or a live-away dad would demand that he have the children every weekend and a night or two during each week.

When parents made demands such as these in my mediation and wouldn't compromise, I felt they were fighting to get back at the other parent rather than to be with their kids. They appeared more angry and demanding than loving and thoughtful, and they would have gotten more of what they wanted by compromising.

Be specific

At the last mediation session I would summarize all the points of agreement the parents had reached, then write them up and mail them to both parents to look over. I asked them to let me know if I accurately reflected what they thought had been agreed upon, and after final adjustments were made, I submitted that agreement to the judge. It became a part of the court ruling, and parents then had a specific and detailed document they could refer to for any future questions about how time or responsibilities were divided.

It was important to be very specific with schedules, particularly when they were fixed. For example, agreements did not just say that dad will have the children from Friday evening to Sunday evening every other weekend. They spelled out exactly what time the children were to be picked up and returned. They were specific about which weekends they referred to. All restrictions and variations were carefully explained in detail.

I always suggested that the weekend portion of the ongoing schedule be changed from "every other weekend" to "the first, third, and fifth weekends of the month." To be completely clear about which ones those were, I defined them as the weekends starting with the first, third, and fifth Fridays of each month.

This arrangement has a couple of advantages. First, it gives the live-away parent four extra weekends annually because there are four months each year that have a fifth Friday in them.

Second, it makes the schedule easily predictable. This is a great advantage. With the schedule of every other weekend, determining parenting-time months in advance is a mistake-prone process of starting with the current date and flipping through the calendar counting alternate weekends month by month. Using the first, third, and fifth weekends allows parents to go directly to the month in question and instantly know who the children will be with; all that parents have to do is look at the first, third, and fifth Fridays of that month. This gives dads and moms the ability to schedule family events, special outings, or anything else, far in advance without mistakes.

Holidays

There are several days each year that parents recognize as special to them. As a mediator I always took the time to build adjustments for these days into the ongoing schedule. Doing so in mediation was sometimes difficult for parents, but it avoided problems later on.

Moms and dads I worked with made specific parenting-time arrangements for holidays such as Christmas, Thanksgiving, Memorial Day, the Fourth of July, and Labor Day. Father's Day, Mother's Day, New Year's, other religious holidays, and their children's birthdays were also occasions for which many parents wanted to make adjustments in the ongoing schedule.

A divorced couple I met with offers a good example of parents working out a Christmas compromise even though that holiday time was important to both of them. They agreed that their two girls would be with their live-in mom, Karen, until about noon on Christmas Day. The children's father, Cary, would then drive ninety-five miles to Karen's, pick them up, and drive them back to his home where they celebrated Christmas with his family later that day. Because their daughters had time off from school for the holidays, they stayed with Cary until New Year's Eve Day when he took them back to their mother's.

This schedule wasn't always easy. Cary didn't enjoy the long drive to Karen's house and back on Christmas, and it presented problems for his extended family's present-opening, dinner, and other traditional holiday celebrations. It was far from perfect for any of these families, but his daughters liked it, and Cary was successful in making it a pleasant experience for his family. If he had complained through the whole thing or continually demanded more, it would have infected the entire experience for the kids and everyone else.

Four ways to handle holidays

There are four primary ways to handle division of holidays, and I present them here. You might use just one or mix and match elements of all four to come up with a schedule that works best for everyone. One way to handle holidays is to alternate them so each parent has a full holiday with the children every other year. An example of this would be dad having his daughter with him on her birthday one year, and her mother having her the next birthday. Another method of handling holidays is to have parents share that holiday every year. In this example, dad might be with his daughter until four P.M. on her birthday each year, and then she would go with her mother for the rest of that day. The third method is for parents to have certain holidays with their children year after year. An example of this would be dad having his daughter every Labor Day and her mom having her every Memorial Day. The fourth option is to make no special arrangements for certain holidays (for example, birthdays and the Fourth of July). In that case, no changes are made in the ongoing schedule for those holidays, and the child celebrates them with whichever parent she happens to be with at the time of the ongoing schedule.

I found, as a mediator, that parents were usually more invested in having certain days or traditions with their children than the kids. I looked with great suspicion at the motives of parents who said they had to have their four- or six-year-old (for example) with them on a birthday or holiday because it was so important to the child. I felt that reflected the parent's needs more than the children's. In most cases, I encouraged arguing parents not to allow children to make decisions about holidays. It put too much pressure on children to side with one parent or the other.

There are two situations, however, when it might be best to allow children to have some say about major holidays. One is with teenagers. Because of their age, they have earned the right to have more control over their lives, and they may have strong preferences in how they spend holidays. The second situation is with children from the ages of about ten to twelve whose parents are recently separated. They have a tradition of doing things one way for several years, and that must be considered when coming up with new holiday schedules.

Younger children will usually go along with whatever timetable parents work out together. For the most part, if younger children are told that it is fun and that they will enjoy it—they will.

It is the responsibility of both parents to come to agreement about holidays and enthusiastically get their kids to like them. It is the live-away dad's job to take his children's feelings and interests into account and provide a pleasant experience for his children on their holidays with him. It is the live-in mom's job to let her children know she agrees with this holiday arrangement and persuade them to see it as an enjoyable one.

Extended time periods

Most parenting-time schedules include extended time periods during which the live-away dad's children stay with him. A fairly common award of time to live-away parents in Wisconsin is two or maybe three weeks each summer and part of Christmas or Easter break.

In my opinion, that is not enough time for parents who want more. A minimum of a month each summer, at least a week during the Christmas school break, and a significant part of the Easter break seems like a better arrangement for both parents and children. It allows children and live-away parents to spend more time together, helps children become more familiar with the live-away parent's house and neighborhood, and gives children a better chance to develop relationships with other young people and adults around the live-away parent.

Keep in mind the needs of children when determining how

these extended time periods will be arranged. It might help to break those times into pieces, especially at first. For example, a month with dad could be divided into four separate weeks, or two periods of two weeks each. Young children, sensitive children, kids in the middle of fighting parents, and kids who have not had much contact with dad will have more difficulty adjusting to separation from home. Introducing the change gradually makes it easier for them to feel comfortable with the live-away parent.

In cases where children have been separated from their live-away parent for a long time, initial contacts may be only a few minutes, then hours, then days. It might not be until the second or third summer that the live-away parent has two weeks or more at a time with the children. Where past contact has been regular, schedules can change much more quickly.

Unfortunately, some moms exaggerate the need for slow change in an effort to put off a dad's contact as long as possible. That is as harmful to children as going too fast, because children and their fathers have a right to be meaningfully involved in each other's lives. The only valid purpose of slow change is to allow children to successfully adapt to time with their father.

If you aren't sure how quickly the increase in extended time should take, listen to the mediator, your attorney if you have one, mental health professionals, and other neutral people you trust. Sometimes slow change may be the best bet. If you insist on moving too quickly, you will create unnecessary resistance in your child's mother. Fair or not, her worries about the change must be taken into consideration. Professionals know from experience that the live-in parent's comfort level with extended-time-period arrangements affects how cooperative she is in complying with them. Remember also that children are strong, but they can be fragile. Rushing them into long visits may cause things to go badly at your home and, therefore, create a difficult experience for your child that could be hard to overcome later. Several months of patience now is not too high a price to pay if it gets you closer to your children for the many years to follow.

With fixed schedules, and to a lesser extent with flexible

schedules, it's important to be specific about how the ongoing schedule, holiday time, and extended time periods affect each other. Let's say, for example, that dad always gets Father's Day with his children, but some years that day falls on a weekend when the ongoing schedule says the kids are with mom. In that case, you may agree in mediation that mom and dad will flip-flop such weekends with the following weekend. Dad will get the Father's Day weekend, and mom will get the next one. Then you are back on the regular schedule.

Be creative and open to compromise when working out scheduling disagreements. You can't prepare for every conflict that might come up, of course, but dealing with the main ones in advance does decrease problems in the future.

The Dozen Keys to Successful Mediation

What you get out of your mediation sessions depends a great deal on how you handle yourself in them. This is also true of custody studies, and although this chapter is about presenting yourself well in parenting-time mediation, the ideas here also will be of great help to you if you are involved in a custody dispute.

To convince a mediator (or a custody evaluator) that you put your children first—and make good decisions for and about them—you must present yourself well. This is easier than many dads realize. You don't have to be a great thinker or speaker. You don't have to wear the right clothes or have the perfect house. You don't have to compete with your former partner. You just have to be yourself. The following keys to successful mediation will show you how to put your best "you" forward.

1. Stay calm

Excessive parental anger was the biggest problem I had to contend with as a mediator. I have spoken in other parts of this book about the need to stay calm, but it's so important I'm doing it again. Except for outright apathy, no parental reaction concerned me more in mediation sessions than unchecked anger.

I support generous parenting-time for live-away parents, and although anger was rarely so strong that it stopped a parent from having time with his child, it did make it much more difficult for me to defend him to the live-in parent or to advocate for anything beyond the minimum. It was difficult to tell a woman that the father of her children, who was yelling at her in my office, is a reasonable person who should have more time with their kids, particularly when that meant more contact with her.

I encourage any father who becomes too angry in mediation, or is afraid he will, to deal with that anger in counseling, in a support group, or some other healthy way so that he can handle that anger more productively.

2. Express your emotions

This key is not contradictory to the previous one about staying calm. You want to express your emotions—but in a safe way. Healthy expression of emotions lies midway between apathy and rage. To me, apathy is not caring, and it shows a lack of concern. Rage may result from too much concern—in other words, misdirected caring. Your kids need your concern but in a safe, calm package.

If you are angry at your children's mom, say so. What feeling person would not be angry or sad in your situation? When you are angry, the mediator already sees it ninety-nine times out of a hundred anyway, so you might as well acknowledge it. Saying that you are mad makes your words fit your actions, making both more powerful and safe. They match. People trust you when you acknowledge your feelings and can express them safely and directly. When you do that you aren't out of control—you're genuine.

Express your thoughts and feelings, but don't lose your temper. You don't have to swear or yell to show people how important the matter is to you. Your words are enough. If you say those words with swearing, yelling, intimidating, or name-calling, you show that your anger is out of control rather than a safe expression of your love.

If you express your emotions by punching your child's mom in the nose in mediation, that is not good. If you say, "I am extremely upset with Sandra because she often changes plans I had with our boys without asking," that is good.

If you swear or shout in session, that is not good. If you say out loud, "I get really frustrated with Sandra sometimes, but I'm working on handling it better because it's important to our kids and us," that is good.

If you call your children's mom names in session, that is not good. If you say, "I get upset because I'm afraid of being pushed out of being a dad. My kids mean a great deal to me, and I know I'm important to them," that is good.

3. Be yourself

Don't try to fool the mediator. Don't try to be who you think the mediator wants you to be. Obviously you want to put your best foot forward, but leave it at that.

Don't compete with your children's mom. You aren't her, you don't talk like her, and you don't act like her. You aren't better, you're just different. Look at what you bring to your kids: firm and fair limits, physical and mental toughness, caring and logical guidance, capacity for rough but safe play, and the opportunity for them to explore their world knowing you will let them fall but not get hurt. Your loving masculine influence on your children is vital to them.

4. Tell the truth

When in doubt tell the truth. Half-truths are too hard to keep track of and will get you in trouble. Most mediators are pretty good at seeing inconsistencies anyway, and although they may not be able to prove lies or gross exaggeration, they know when something is up. Because the stakes are so high in mediation, parents are reluctant to tell the truth if it may put them in a less than perfect light, but mediators look for integrity in parents, and it only takes a couple of slips on your part for them to doubt your credibility.

Telling the truth doesn't mean you have to blast people either. We all have feelings, so if you point out what you consider a fault in your child's mom, be diplomatic about it. I've seen some dads become self-righteous with facts, as if nothing else mattered. Some dads are really cold in their criticism, and that makes them look angry and distant. You don't have to be all gushy and apologetic with what you say, but say it with a respect for how your words affect others.

5. Know your kids

Know your children well. What foods do they like and dislike? What games do they like to play? If they are in school, what are their teachers like? What are their favorite classes? Do they have pets? What animals do they like? What do they want to be when they grow up? (Okay, forget that one, it changes every month.)

If you have more than one child, how are they different, and how are they the same? What kind of personality does each one have? What are they good at? Is your daughter quiet, thoughtful, outgoing, adventurous? Is your son confident, curious, gentle, active? What scares your child, makes her mad, makes him sad, or makes her happy?

The better you know your children, the better you will look in mediation. But, even more important, you'll know your kids better, and what's the point of being part of their lives if not to enjoy them and know about them? To find out more about your kids, talk with them—but don't grill them. Think about the real interest you have in their lives. Think about how much fun it is to learn more about them.

One way to get children talking is to tell them about yourself and what you did as a kid. If they are interested in your stories, they'll probably interrupt you and want to tell about themselves. Let them. Have fun with this. Settle into a relaxed space. Be a good listener.

Avoid the temptation to judge what your kids say as good or bad. If you start judging, they'll stop talking. Remember, this is not an interview—it's a conversation. Also be sure in this conversation that you don't ask them about their mother. If you do, they will rightfully wonder what your real interest is in talking with them.

Your kids are not adults, and they don't talk like adults. Younger children communicate more with playing than talking, so play freely with them. Older kids may never get to the point, never solve the problem, and come out with the goofiest stuff, but that's how they sometimes talk. Go with it, or they'll stop. Be interested, or they'll stop.

You don't, by the way, have to reel off an inventory of your child's interests to the mediator. The point of these discussions with your children is get to know them better, and when you do that you'll be prepared to talk more comfortably in mediation.

6. Stick to the point

As a mediator, one of the most frustrating parts of my work was keeping parents on the subject. I constantly found myself leading them back from tangents they couldn't leave behind, whether that was angry stories of what was done to them, proof of their points, or defensive reactions to the other parent. All of these paths led us away from solving the problems at hand.

Stick to the point that the mediator is addressing. If you are angry or hurt about things that come up in session, acknowledge your thoughts out loud, but be careful that they don't take over the session.

7. Look at your own behavior

It's very easy to focus on the behavior of your child's mom. But the purpose of mediation is to reach agreement on parenting issues, not find fault with her—even if she is full of fault. If your child's mother has so many flaws that she's a destructive parent, fight for your child in a custody proceeding. If, for whatever reasons, you are not going to dispute custody, stick to the purpose of mediation, which is to iron out scheduling and related problems.

Look at yourself and your behavior. When you disagree with your child's mom, it's important for you to speak up, but if you constantly focus on her, it will backfire. You will look like the unreasonable parent. Focusing on yourself, on the other hand, makes you a person who takes responsibility for his actions and meets his child's needs.

8. Talk about your former partner's strengths and your own

I often saw dads in mediation credit their children's moms as good and caring parents. I was very impressed by that. It builds trust and creates a positive atmosphere in mediation. But some dads are reluctant to talk about their own strengths, either because they feel like they're bragging or they haven't looked closely at what their strengths are. But enough of that attitude. It's important to know and talk about your strengths during mediation.

Before you go to mediation, think about what you bring to your children as their father: consistent discipline, important values, sensitivity, warmth, respect for others, the value of hard work, active play, firm limits, a feeling of safety, encouragement of exploration, skills in sports (or reading or music), expertise with tools, love of nature, and a desire to achieve.

It's important for the mediator to know what you think your parenting strengths are. Part of mediation is making a case that you improve the life of your child, and to do that you have to bring up your strong points. If you don't, they may not come out. The fourth key was about telling the truth. This is about the whole truth, and that means not just weak points but strengths as well.

9. Put the kids ahead of your anger

In mediation (and other times for that matter) assess whether you are pushing a point to meet your children's needs or because you are frustrated with their mother. This is often a tough task, but anger and frustration will cloud your judgment if you aren't careful, so do your best to handle those emotions effectively. Keep your mind on what your children need from you.

Remember that your frustration is your responsibility, not your children's or their mother's. You are the only one who can channel it effectively, and no matter how difficult that is, you can do it.

10. Answer questions fully

Mediation is an opportunity for you to show why you want to be a meaningful part of your children's lives and what you are doing, and will do, to make that happen. Tell the mediator and your children's mom what you enjoy about being with your kids. This might sound ridiculously obvious—of course you like being with your kids—but sometimes things just have to be said out loud for people to understand.

If you have not been with your kids as much as you'd like because of conflicts with their mother or for any other reasons, it is particularly important that you express your thoughts and desires in words. Explain why you have not been as involved as you wish you had, and talk about how you see your involvement with them in the future.

Be sure to talk about at least a couple of the most important things about your relationship with your kids. If you aren't sure what to say, ask people close to you what they think is important about you, your children, and your involvement with them. Talk about these points in mediation, and don't sell yourself short.

This reminds me of the way I wrote papers in high school and college. When the class was given an assignment, we were always told how many pages it must be, so, of course, I made sure it was that length and no more. If we had to write ten pages, I'd be done with what I thought was the important stuff in about three, then I'd fill in the next seven with "fluff."

It was not until about my third year in college that something dawned on me. All that "fluff" that teachers and professors asked me to write was actually important information! It wasn't just filling. It was what they were looking for! It was what they wanted me to learn and explain, and they knew that if they didn't make me write more than I would have on my own, I'd never get to it. I'd never fully express important points. Express yourself fully in mediation. Don't go on and on in sessions, but present your thoughts and feelings fully.

11. Admit your mistakes

If you goofed, say so. Take responsibility for it, and try to do better next time. We all make mistakes, and mediators know that. If you made a mistake, explain what happened, and be open to questions about it if there are any. Tell the mediator why it happened, how you feel about your actions, acknowledge the right of others to be upset, and tell what actions you are taking to see that it doesn't happen again.

12. Compromise

I encourage all parents to work toward compromise. Refusing to change only saps the strength of parents and kids. Your children need you to get along with their mother, and if that often means giving in, so be it. I don't mean caving in, giving up everything and walking away. I mean decrease the fighting between you and your former partner by compromising.

Always be open to the mediator's suggestions and feedback about compromise. His or her comments might really help, and change on your part shows that you can be flexible in and out of mediation sessions.

In the sessions I conducted, compromise rarely came easily, but almost all parents were eventually able to reach a workable solution. Seldom were both parents totally happy with the compromise, but at least it was *their* compromise and not conditions placed upon them by the judge.

When you decide to involve the courts in your parenting disputes, do so wisely. Use the information I've presented here to help you decide when to make use of the legal system and how to present yourself to professionals. You can deal with the court individually to improve your specific situation, or you can band together with other live-away dads and moms trying to change the laws and practices of divorce and family courts statewide and nationwide.

Courts are a powerful tool for live-away dads and their children when parents are not capable of working together. Unfortunately, the court process also can be agonizingly ineffective. So use the system sparingly. Be realistic about what you can expect to get from the court process, and try hard to work out problems with your child's mother before you get the system involved.

Keep in mind that the court system has many faults, but it is not the enemy. There are many court workers, attorneys, judges, and other professionals who do their jobs well, as well as some who don't, but they are not against you. Do your best, therefore, to work with them, not against them.

If you are suspicious and hostile with these professionals and believe they are only out for the money or intentionally unfair, that will show in your attitude, and it will not help you. If you come to believe that they are trying to do a good job under difficult circumstances—and if you deal with them objectively and calmly even if you strongly disagree with them—you will be much more likely to succeed. If you enter the court system, do so with eyes that look inward as well as outward.

PART IV

Fathering Your Children

Live-away dads' special life circumstances involve brief periods of intense fathering of their children separated by longer periods of time away from them. This can be extremely challenging, but your presence in your children's lives is exceedingly important. Don't let physical distance stop you from sharing your fathering gifts.

The role that men have most often been assigned in families is that of "breadwinner" or "protector." Many of us were not raised to fully understand our importance as nurturers to our children. Too often we allowed or expected our children's mother to be the primary nurturer with our kids.

But you can get more involved in fathering even from a distance. When you are alone with your children you are free to parent in your own masculine style. You may develop a relationship with your children that is deeper and more satisfying than ever.

CHAPTER 11

Living Apart but Growing Together: Communicating with Your Kids

"If men do not keep on speaking terms with children, they cease to be men, and become merely machines for eating and for earning money."   —JOHN UPDIKE

"To cease to be loved is for the child practically synonymous with ceasing to live."   —KARL A. MENNINGER

There were times when I struggled to stay in touch with my daughters from one hundred and ten miles away. I remember one phone call I made to them when they were about nine and eleven years old. My oldest answered, and right away she said, "Dad, we gotta go. There's a really good show on TV."

I was having a particularly bad day before that call. Now I was really upset. Crushed. I wanted to yell at her, to hurt both my daughters for not taking my feelings into account, again. But I got off the phone calmly, doing my best not to let them know how bad I felt.

My girls went happily back to the television. I sat alone in my apartment where I yelled out loud, "Why can't they ever appreciate me? How can they watch that stupid TV and be so selfish? I can't believe this! Don't they have any idea how much I do for them? Don't they care at all how hard I work to stay connected to them? Don't they know how hard this is for me?"

Of course, the answer to these questions is "No, they don't know how hard this is for me." And they shouldn't. It is my job as a father to understand my children's needs and put them ahead of my own. As hurt as I was, they should not feel guilty about enjoying their day. They didn't do anything wrong. Venting my anger at them would only have made things worse. They were just being kids. I had to allow them to be kids.

Tune in carefully to your children to help them deal with your separation. Expect different children to have varied reactions, and be careful not to assume that the quiet or well-behaved child needs less attention than others. Young children tend to blame themselves for a separation. Children a few years older may react with great sadness and have difficulty eating or sleeping or become highly emotional, clingy, or unusually defiant. Teens may react to divorce or separation by spending more time in their rooms or by becoming disrespectful, rude, moody, confused, relieved, or distant—and that's just in one day!

As difficult as it may be for children to adjust to a parent leaving, all is not lost. The emotional challenges brought on by divorce provide an opportunity for children to learn more about themselves and their strengths, just as it does for adults, and you can help them get through their struggles by caring and listening.

Helping Your Children Deal with the Breakup

When you talk to your children about your separation, realize that doing so is a process, not an event. You can't just sit them down once and tell them everything. Make yourself available when they want to talk to you, listen to them in nondefensive and nonjudgmental ways, and be patient when they misbehave. Misbehaving may be the best way they know to get their emotions out. Supporting your words with your actions is also important. Don't just tell your children you are there for them, actually be there.

Four Things Kids Need to Hear
from Their Parents about the Breakup

Children whose parents separate usually have many worries about what's going to happen to them, but their fears can be diminished if they hear the four messages in this section. When possible, it's best for parents to deliver these messages together, because joint delivery will help children believe and accept what is being said. If arguments between parents make a shared presentation impossible, the next best thing is for both parents to agree to give the same messages separately. If that isn't possible, at least be sure that *you* say these things to your children.

1. Your mom and I are breaking up with each other—not you

Assume that your children have no idea what your breakup with their mother means. Starting from that point, let them know that it means separation of parents, not divorce of children. Clarify that you and their mom are changing your relationship with each other, not breaking up with them, and remind them as often as you need to that your separation from their mother does not mean you care less about them.

Just as children may fear what will happen to them when a parent leaves the home, they may imagine they can get you back together. A certain amount of that thinking is normal for children and not automatically harmful. If, however, your child spends a lot of time thinking about getting you back together or trying to do so, you may have to gently remind her at times that she cannot. As you tell your child this, remember that part of her anxiety may be fears that she will lose you, so be sure to remind her that you are separating from her mother, not her.

2. The breakup is not your fault

Children sometimes blame themselves when parents separate. Make it clear to your children that they did not cause the breakup in any way. It is particularly important that you say this if your relationship with their mother included conflict over your children. Kids who hear parents arguing about them are more likely to believe that they are somehow responsible for the split. Let your children know that your relationship ended because both parents could not get along with each other and that it was not their fault.

3. We both love you

Children need to know they are loved by both parents, and it is best if they hear that message from parents together—not just mom saying, "I love you," and dad saying, "I love you," but mom saying, "I love you and your dad loves you," and dad saying, "I love you and your mom loves you." See the difference? When you tell your children that they are loved by you and their mother you actually tell them three things: (1) that you love your children, (2) that their mother loves them, and (3) that you want them to love their mother.

Without your approval of their love for their mother, it's hard for your kids to fully relax around you. Instead, they become self-conscious about their behavior and afraid to express themselves freely. And you need to affirm their mother's love for them regardless of what she says about you, because it's a message they need to get regardless of what other messages they hear. You can't change or make up for what other people say. You can only do what is right for your kids and yourself.

If mistrust and conflict between you and your children's mother is so strong that you find it impossible to tell your kids she loves them, at least let them know you love them. If you can't get yourself to say positive things about her, at least avoid negative statements.

4. I will always be there for you

It's vital that your children know you will be there for them—forever. Actually, all kids need to hear this from their parents, but when they live apart from you it's even more important.

Your kids need to know that they will remain an important part of your life even though they will not see you as often. Not that you will solve every problem they have—but that you will guide them as they solve their own. Not that you will endlessly bail them out of trouble—but that you will never give up on them. Not that you will always be right—but that you will always be right there when they need you.

Show your children you will always be there by being on time, by always calling when you say you will, and by following through on every commitment you make. Being there for them means not just what you do but how you do it. Listen to them, stay calm, and accept them for who they are. Try to tell them in words that you will always be there. Don't assume they know something if you haven't told them. Showing them is critical, but telling them makes it crystal clear.

In the years after my divorce, there were many times that I told my daughters I loved them. When my oldest daughter, Chris, was twenty-one, she told me that one of the most meaningful things I had ever said to her was that I loved her unconditionally. I remember it too. It happened in the driveway of her mom's house when she was eight years old. I had just driven her and her younger sister, Kyla, there after a weekend with them. Before they got out of the car I turned to them and said, "I want you to know something. I love you unconditionally." They looked at me quizzically, and knowing they didn't understand, I went on, "Do you know what 'unconditionally' means?"

In unison they replied, "No."

I continued, "It means that no matter how old you are, what you do, or where you are—I love you. That's all there is to it. Nothing will ever stop me from loving you. Period." As they listened quietly, I continued, "I just want you to know that. I don't always tell you what I'm thinking, so I thought this time I would. Okay?"

"Okay, Dad," said Chris.

"Yeah, Dad," said Kyla.

"Great," I said. "Now, I gotta get going. Have a great week in school. I'll call you next weekend. Love you."

"Okay, Dad," said Kyla as she opened the door.

"I love you too," said Chris as they scrambled out of the car.

That's all that happened. Yet it was so powerful that my daughter never forgot it.

Four Ways to Talk with Your Kids about Your Separation

I've just presented four things that every child of divorce or separation needs to hear. Now I'd like to give you some guidance on *how* to talk with your children. These four suggestions will give you the ability to tell them what you need to without saying too little or too much.

1. Tell your children the truth at a level they can understand

There may be times you start conversations with your kids about your separation and times that your children come to you with questions (how often they come to you depends partially upon how caring your responses are). In either case, it is best to avoid detail, especially with younger children. There are many adult things they don't need to hear.

Keep conversations with your children simple and brief as you pay attention to whether they want to keep talking. Check in with them by asking something like, "Are you doing okay?" or "Do you have any more questions?" Don't be afraid of questions they have. You don't have to have the "right" answers, just be a good listener.

If you really feel stuck with a question—join the club. We all have that problem at times. Keep in mind that your children are usually less concerned about getting an exact answer than they are in knowing that they will be okay in this family disruption and that they can express themselves freely around you. If a question does stump you, tell your child you will have to think about it a while and get back to him or her. Then ask someone you trust what they would say, and go back to your child and finish the discussion.

Older teenagers have the capacity to understand relationships better than young children, so you may decide to be more open with them about your separation, but be sure your conversations are to help your children deal with their lives, not to get them to side with you. Regardless of how mature your children are, they are not yet part of the adult world, and care must be taken to avoid dragging them into it.

A divorced dad I worked with, Mark, had a son and daughter who lived almost two hundred miles away with their mother. Both children had frequent conflicts with their mother and, in their early teens, began to tell Mark about them. Before that, Mark hadn't known much about what their mother was like in her home. He knew there were many problems, but she refused to talk about them. He suspected that she was often in bars and that his children had few consistent rules and inadequate supervision, but he never questioned his kids about these things, because he didn't want to put them in the middle.

Mark's children were failing in school, had problems with friends, and had experienced minor contacts with the police. They were really starting to think of themselves as bad kids. Mark wanted his kids to take responsibility for their actions, but he didn't want them to blame themselves for things that he believed were a result of the way their mother parented. When his daughter began to open up to him about the way things were going at home, Mark realized they were old enough to hear some of his concerns.

He talked about some of the frustrations he'd had with their mother—many of them the same ones his kids experienced. He talked about his fears for them and how he felt their mother's behavior affected them. He helped them understand their situation without cutting their mother down by sharing the truth without blaming. Before Mark's conversations with his kids, they didn't know how their mother's drinking and absences from home were affecting them. They just thought they were bad, and they needed to know that they weren't.

Mark got no pleasure from telling his kids about their mother's shortcomings. He told them because they needed to understand the effects of their mother's drinking upon them. He had these discussions with his kids not because he wanted them to hate their mother, but because he wanted them to love themselves.

2. Avoid complaints about their mother

Children don't need to know the mistakes their mother made, and complaining about her gives your kids adult information they can't understand. This may cause them to act out in school, develop stomach problems, withdraw, or in some other way express their hurt and confusion.

If you want to share with your children some of the things you did that you regret, that may be a good idea, but don't complain about their mother. Acknowledging some of your errors—with emotion but without feeling sorry for yourself or blaming your children's mother—allows your children to see that you are fair about what's going on. That promotes trust between you and your children, and it helps them see you as human.

3. Share your feelings with your kids

If you want your children to open up to you, open up to them. With older kids, that may evolve into long discussions, and with young children it may be as simple as saying something like, "Yes, daddy is sad right now too." Every dad expresses himself in different ways, but being the strong silent type with your kids just doesn't cut it. Let them see your emotions at times. That way they'll know you are real and that it's okay for them to express their emotions.

It's okay to occasionally let your children know you are upset— just don't lose your cool when you do it. That will only scare them. Find other outlets for those strong emotions, including friends, a support group, writing, exercise, or other positive activities so that you can talk calmly to your children.

If you're not sure what to talk about with your kids, try to imagine what you would be thinking and feeling if you were going through exactly what they are. Talk about that. Don't assume your kids have no questions because they ask none. Every once in a while ask your children if they have any questions about what is going on. If they do, answer them briefly and simply.

In all of this, remember that the emotions behind your children's questions are usually more important than the questions themselves. This is not a work environment where you search for solutions to problems with the goal of achieving measurable outcomes—this is children and their emotional needs being met.

Don't get upset with yourself if your responses to your children are not as skilled as you'd like. Go from where you are right now, and make that better. It doesn't matter where you start. You can always improve.

If you have a little voice in the back of your head (or perhaps a blaring voice) telling you that you sometimes handle emotions poorly, don't get down on yourself. You are not alone. Emotional mess ups are much more common than you probably think. You just don't get the chance to see them often. As a therapist, I see it all the time, even in the most together-looking people you could imagine.

4. Listen to your children

Divorce shakes your children's worlds, and it's natural for them to be afraid, resentful, sad, or confused. Allow them to express those feelings. Listen to them without judgment, criticism, or attempts to fix their problem. Also encourage them to talk to relatives, teachers, coaches, counselors, or close friends of yours. That gives them a different perspective that may be very helpful.

We men are often more likely to give solutions than listen, even when solutions aren't requested. Trying to help others solve a problem is certainly important, but many times the best thing we can do for our children is just listen and accept what they say. When we rush in with answers, try to take away the pain, or attempt to convince them that everything will be all right, they don't feel understood. So just listen. Keep eye contact. Don't fidget. Give them your undivided attention. If you want to jump in with solutions, bite your tongue.

I know a dad named Marvin whose ability to listen turned a sad moment into a happy one. He and his wife were divorced when their daughter, Melissa, was eight years old. One night about a year after that Melissa was at her dad's house, and he noticed that she was very quiet. After a while he decided to say something about it.

As she sat in front of him he gently massaged her shoulders for a few minutes and then asked if there was anything she wanted to talk about. She started to cry. He was quite surprised by her reaction, but he stayed quiet, and she began to talk. She told him she was thinking about her mom a lot and wishing all three of them were together like the family they used to be.

Marvin continued to listen without offering solutions. He had wondered before if she would ever talk about those feelings. He feared she never would or wouldn't until she was in her twenties. Marvin told me that was a special night for both of them, and ever since then they've felt a bit closer to each other.

Five Things You Can Do to Make Your Child's Life— and Yours—Better

So far in this chapter we have talked about what to *say* to your children and how to say it. Now we'll look at five things you can *do* to promote a successful relationship with them. It's not easy to make the best parenting choice every time. Sometimes you don't know what to do when problems come up, and sometimes you know exactly what to do but are too upset to do it. This section provides five ways to conduct yourself that always help. When you're not sure what to do or not do, you can know that these five actions are always beneficial.

1. Keep your promises to your children

Your children depend on you for their physical and emotional needs. When you make a promise to them, you need to follow through. Your kept promises are an important source of stability for your child in an unpredictable world.

Every time you tell your children you will do something—pick them up for the weekend, call at six P.M., go to their school play, read them a bedtime story, help them with homework, or play a game—but don't follow through, you give them a little wound. You diminish their ability to trust just a tiny little bit, the way that many of us were wounded by our fathers or mothers.

To avoid those wounds with your children, take responsibility for thinking before you speak. Make sure you can do something before you promise it. If you're not absolutely sure you can follow through because of your schedule, finances, the weather, or anything else, tell that to your child in advance.

In the rare case where a promise can't be kept, be prepared for an emotional overreaction by your children. Change, and that includes the cancellation of plans they had counted on, can be very upsetting to kids. If you must break a promise, tell your kids why you can't follow through, and be understanding if they react strongly.

Most of us would never consider breaking a promise to a boss; yet we sometimes allow our promises to our kids to go by the wayside. We convince ourselves that more important adult things got in the way. But you know what? There are no more important adult things than keeping our word to our children. Jobs can be replaced. Children can't. Think before you speak, and always keep your promises.

2. Let your children know in words and deeds that you will be okay

For children to feel confident and capable, they must believe that you are. If they see that you are devastated by the separation, they'll fear for their own emotional safety. They may show this by becoming overly attached to people, angry, withdrawn, or they might try to parent you.

It is reasonable to let your children, especially older kids, see that you are hurting at times (they can see it anyway), but you must also let them know in your actions, and in your words, that you will be all right in spite of your struggles. That allows them to focus on childhood challenges that are important to them while you take care of the adult things.

3. Support their mother

Don't cut your children's mother down even if she says unfair or untrue things about you. Cutting her down lowers you in the long run. If she makes mistakes in her life, your kids will eventually see that for themselves. They don't need you pointing out her errors.

Support her parenting, and cooperate with her as much as you can. When you do disagree with her, do it in private, away from the kids. Children don't need one parent they love putting down the other parent they love. It only makes their pain worse.

4. Parent your kids the best you can when you are with them

You have little control over what your children's mother does in her parenting. All you can do is parent the best you can when your children are with you. Do not alter your parenting to make up for what you think your children's mom is doing wrong in hers.

Effective parenting includes firm and fair limits, patience, understanding, communication, and a lot of other skills in just the right amounts. It is not a case of "more is better." If she's too lenient, it doesn't help for you to be too strict. If she runs around doing too much for your kids, it doesn't help things if you do too little. Children need balanced parenting from you when they are with you, and if you stray from that balance in an attempt to make up for mistakes by your child's mother, more harm is done than good.

5. Stay involved over the long haul

Be in your children's lives for the long haul. I cannot emphasize this enough. Don't allow problems to sidetrack your long-term goal of a close relationship. Stay as closely connected as you can.

I know a dad named Jack, who has two daughters. He and his former wife, Susan, are both professionals. They were married for about ten years, but after numerous separations, they were finally divorced. Susan was very antagonistic after the separation. She constantly changed plans he made with the kids and caused his contact with them to be completely unpredictable. She frequently went back to court for more child support, including one occasion when she did so less than two months after they had finally reached yet another court-ordered agreement. She hired and fired four divorce attorneys in three years. In spite of these challenges, Jack consistently spent time with his daughters through the years.

Susan also had difficulty getting along with their children, especially when they became teenagers. Jack strongly disagreed with the way Susan dealt with their daughters, but he did not want to undermine her authority with them or put their girls in the middle, so he didn't argue with her in front of the children or speak badly about her. Things continued to get worse at Susan's home, however, and when their oldest daughter, Jodi, was sixteen, her mother told her to leave the house and she moved in with her dad. One year later, Jack's other daughter, Leah, who was then fourteen, moved in with him as well. She had run away from her mom's house several times because of the problems there, and Jack had always returned her home, but one day she ran to the police station rather than his house. When that happened, Jack had had enough. He started proceedings in court and was awarded full custody of Leah.

I don't want this story to create false hopes for live-away dads. Few of us will be in Jack's position, and we can't know what the future holds for us and our kids, but being a positive part of our children's lives means being there for them when they need us for the small things or the big things.

Do your best to stay involved with your children on a regular basis and over the long haul. Even if your pain causes you to see your kids less for a while, keep the lines of communication open if possible, including phone calls, letters, or E-mail. They don't have to be lengthy and brilliant conversations or literary masterpieces, just communicate one way or another so your kids know you think of them.

If, for any reason, you haven't seen your children for months or even years, it's never too late to get involved in their lives again. Longer separations will probably require more patience in reuniting, but it is never too late. If you have had a long absence, don't expect to take up where you left off. Your children must become accustomed to your reinvolvement and so must their mother. This could take many months or more. Part of that readjustment is time for them to develop a trust that they will not be separated from you again.

I've met several troubled dads who made many promises to their children that they did not keep. Some of them would go months or years with little or no contact with their children and were often demanding and negative. Some were angry at their children for not calling them or appreciating them enough.

After a while, I began to see that these dads had one thing in common; not one of them had a good relationship with his own dad as a child. Many carried great anger at their fathers. I've had two fathers calmly tell me they'd never forgive their dads for the verbal and emotional abuse their fathers had filled their childhoods with, even if they asked for forgiveness on their deathbeds.

Fortunately, most of us weren't hurt that badly. But many of us had fathers who couldn't freely show their love. How well do you think your dad prepared you to father your children lovingly?

As difficult as it may be, the responsibility for communication between you and your children is yours, not theirs, regardless of their age. Most children, and that includes teenagers, simply do not have the emotional maturity to communicate effectively with parents despite how much they love us, how important we think it is that they communicate, or how much we do for them. That's part of the definition of being a child or teenager.

At times we may feel totally unappreciated by our kids, but it is our job as adults to keep positive contact going in spite of it. We must see our importance to our children even when it doesn't seem like they do.

Keep a Healthy Balance

Contact with your children requires a balanced approach to life. I had a client, Vince, who hurt his relationship with his four-, six-, and nine-year-old sons by forcing contact with them. After eleven years of marriage, Vince was divorced and moved out of the home. At first the exchange of his sons seemed to go okay, but strong conflicts soon developed between him and his children's mom, Pam, and, after a while, she refused to allow the kids to see him.

For three months after that Vince drove to his former home at his scheduled pick-up time, parked his car outside, and either waited there throughout the parenting-time or drove off and returned again at the drop-off time. He did this twice a week, week after week, knowing each time that his children could not come out.

I'm not sure why he did this. Maybe it was an effort to show his children he loved them. Maybe he did it to wear Pam down so she'd let the kids come out. Maybe it was an angry response to the powerlessness he felt. Whatever his reasons, the results for him and his children were not positive.

It must have been extremely painful for Vince to sit out there in his car alone, with his children so close but unavailable. It also must have been confusing and upsetting for his kids. Here they were, stuck between their mother who would not allow them to go out their front door to be with their father and their dad who was sitting alone in a car fifty feet away, day after day after day. What an emotional pull for those kids. They were quite literally in the middle.

I know both these parents loved their kids, but neither was making good decisions. They could have worked it out together through direct discussion or an agreement to go to mediation. If Pam refused to cooperate, Vince could have backed down from this confrontation to let things cool off. He could have tried writing a letter to her to explain his concerns, or he could have requested mediation services himself, and the court would have required Pam to attend. There were many things he could have done that would not have put his sons in the middle, but he didn't.

Do what's best for your child, regardless of what your child's mom does. Requests or demands that she do something are a waste of your time if she doesn't want to cooperate. Fair or unfair, that's the way it is. If you do what needs to be done, you help your child. Someone needs to do what's "right" for your child. If she won't, you had better, or nobody will.

Another client I had, Charles, told me how difficult it was for him when he ended his six-year, live-in relationship with Gail, his son's mother. After he moved out of the house, he was completely lost. He felt abandoned, angry, and confused. Nothing seemed important to him, except his son. It was his commitment to his son that pulled Charles through.

Knowing that he had to keep himself together for his son helped Charles out of his loneliness and confusion. When he put his son's needs ahead of his own, he felt he had something else to live for rather than just himself. As he put it, "If I was feeling miserable, it didn't mean the whole world was miserable."

There were many times that Charles was angry at Gail. She moved frequently and exposed their young son to numerous boyfriends. She didn't follow through on her commitments to her son and seemed to set up arguments with Charles. But he stayed involved and kept his son out of the middle.

Charles even changed his career direction. He had just gotten his teacher's license when he and Gail broke up. He was going to be a high school teacher, but he learned that the parochial school his son was entering needed a teacher for his class. He immediately altered his goal of becoming a high school teacher in a public school and took the much lower paying job teaching his son's elementary school class.

It wasn't the direction he ever thought he'd take, but he wanted to stay close to his son and did what it took to do so. Like Vince, Charles had plenty of anger, but unlike Vince, he channeled it constructively. He kept his son out of the middle by changing himself, and it worked out beautifully.

Communicate, Communicate, Communicate

Another live-away dad I worked with, Joe, communicated with his young daughters regularly and had creative ways of expressing himself. He wrote them a little song about how much he loved them, and when they stayed with him he sang it to them at night. He drew and sent them a picture of where he lived even though they had been there many times. He told them over and over the stories of how he had cried in happiness at their birth, how proud their mother was of them, and all the visitors they'd had in the hospital. When the girls stayed at his house, as he put them to bed he'd ask them who loved them. Then he'd help them think of their grandparents, their mother, himself, friends, relatives, teachers, other people they wanted to name, and even their pets.

After my divorce, I wrote and called my daughters regularly. Before they were old enough to read, I sent them pictures I drew. Often our phone conversations were just a few minutes long. It was almost always me who called or wrote. But they knew I was thinking of them. We were living apart but growing together.

As their lives evolved so did our conversations. In the early years I heard a lot about teachers and playing with friends. I knew how important these things were to them at that age so I listened. As they grew up, our conversations slowly turned into intimate discussions about fears, triumphs, drugs, sex, relationships, boy-friends, college, and countless other things of importance to them.

I know another dad who mailed audiotape messages to his children instead of letters. Marvin, whom I wrote about earlier, went on vacation for a week once and sent his daughter a postcard every day. He tells me she has saved them. Another dad I know left brief messages for his kids on the answering machine in their house. Another had a friend make a doll for his daughter that she slept with at her mother's house.

We've talked a lot in this chapter about how to father your kids: what to say to them, how to say it, and how to interact with them. You can use these ideas whether you are just beginning the process of separation or have been apart for years. Fathering is a lifelong responsibility. Loving your child and changing yourself to be an even healthier parent is within your power. If you want to improve your relationship with your children, you can. I've seen many men do it.

CHAPTER 12

Creating a Kid-Friendly Home

"When I grow up I want to be a little boy."
—JOSEPH HELLER

I n this chapter we'll take a fun look at ways to enjoy your time with your kids. We'll explore some challenges your children and you face when you become involved with a new partner and her family. We'll then look at the physical setup and emotional atmosphere of your home, fun stuff to do with your kids, a surprising rule for games, and how to be a glad dad.

Help Your Children Adjust to Your New Partner

If you have gotten involved with someone else after your children's mother, realize that your kids have quite an adjustment to make. They may blame her for your breakup, be angry at her for taking your time from them, think she's trying to replace their mom, or, at the other extreme, become very attached to her. To protect your children from unnecessary emotional turmoil, be sure not to be bring a new woman into your children's lives unless your relationship with her is serious.

Your live-away children have to get along with not only your new partner but her children, if any, and other relatives of hers. If the two of you have new children together, more relationships are started.

Because of the physical separation between you and your live-away children, they may need reassurance that you still love them. If they see you setting up a new family, they may wonder if they are still included in your life. Be sure you tell them that new people in your life will never replace them. Communicate with your children regularly, and remind them in words and actions that you love them wherever they are and whatever they do. Involve them in your new family's activities (teenagers may not always want to join, but make the offer). Take time to be with your children alone, and be attentive to their feelings.

Your children may not know how to tell you their thoughts, so don't assume that everything is okay simply because everything looks fine on the surface. Observe your children's behavior closely. Notice how they get along with these new people in their life. Check it out with them once in a while by asking how they are getting along with your new partner or her family.

If your child's mom, your new partner, or others express concerns about your children's adjustment, take them seriously. If they have suggestions about ways to help your children adapt more successfully, listen. Patience and a true sensitivity to the needs of your live-away children will help them a lot as they adjust to the changes in their lives.

Live-Away Kids and the New Kids: Getting Along

It's frustrating for you if your live-away children can't get along with your new partner's kids or your new biological children. But it can be awfully tough on the kids as well. Your live-away children and the new children in your life may be jealous, angry, playful, cooperative, afraid, sad, or happy. They may fight over bedrooms, toys, chores, computer space, time and attention of parents, friendships, loyalties, television shows, space at the kitchen table, and who gets the bathroom first. Hopefully they'll also play together, learn from each other, laugh, share, work cooperatively with each other, and make close friendships.

Encourage all these children to work things out together. Be a good role model by calmly resolving conflicts with your children's mom and your new partner. Have family meetings in your new home during which your live-away children and the other kids are allowed to respectfully express their feelings and come to agreement on problems that come up.

Be patient with them. Adjustments can take a long time, and children must go at their own pace. When upset with them, take a minute to think about how you might feel—and how you would like to be treated—if you were that child. Remember that you can't make them get along no matter what you do. You can, however, encourage and support them as you help them generate ideas about ways to do things differently. Talk with them about choices, and give them opportunities to problem-solve with your guidance.

Never play favorites. Go out of your way to see that you treat the children fairly and equally whether they are your live-away children, your new partner's children, or your new biological children. Also find opportunities to make each one of them feel special as an individual. Kids are extremely attuned to fairness and equality. They notice which children have the most money spent on them for Christmas, who has the most chores, and if they are all disciplined the same or not. Be very attentive to these things.

Appreciate the adjustments your children have to make, and be sure to work with your new partner on ways to resolve discord between the kids. Look for, and talk about, what works rather than what doesn't. Try to come up with solutions that she and you can fully support. Consider your children's conflicts to be opportunities for you and your new partner to creatively work together.

Physical Setup

Take a quick look at the physical setup of your home. It doesn't matter if you live in your own home, a friend's house, a small apartment, or a huge mansion—you want to create a safe and comfortable environment for your kids in the space you have.

Safe environment

A safe environment is one in which your child will not be physically or emotionally harmed. This includes protection from tumbles down the stairs, rules about playing outside, and care with tools, knives, toxic household cleaners, medicine cabinet pills, and the kitchen stove.

Safety also means not requiring your child to sit on strange Uncle Joe's lap or to kiss Aunt Sally who drinks a bit too much. It means being observant not only of your child's friends but of all the adults they are around.

Your child—of any age—can be taken advantage of by adults. Be very careful about who you have in your home, who baby-sits for your child, and who you allow around your children even for brief periods of time. Only have people there that you trust totally. Ask yourself if you would be completely and absolutely safe around these people if you were just five, ten, or fifteen years old. If you can't say "yes," never leave your children alone with them.

Comfortable environment

A comfortable physical environment is one in which your children feel at ease and relaxed. Their need for a comfortable space is as important to them as yours is to you. Does it matter to you how your room, apartment, or house is set up? Think about the details. Look around your place right now. If someone came in and told you to put your furniture where he wanted it, to get rid of your television, to turn the heat up, or paint the walls pink, what would you do?

Do you have (or have you had in the past) a garage or basement workroom, shop, office, or other private space? Does it matter to you what tools are in there or how things are arranged? If so, you can see how it is for kids. They may not have the sophisticated needs of grown-ups or the skills to complete complex adult projects, but they do have needs and wants that are extremely important to them at their level.

To be close to your children, recognize their needs. I don't mean give them everything they want whenever they want it. I mean give them choices and control when those choices don't directly endanger their safety or moral development.

As far as the physical setup of your place goes, your children's sleeping area may be the most important part of the house. Whether they have their own room, share a room with siblings, or have other arrangements, this is a place for privacy when possible and for familiarity with surroundings.

When my kids were small I rented a one-bedroom apartment. They slept on the floor of my living room when they stayed with me. Ideally they would have had their own rooms, but I couldn't afford it. To make it more comfortable and fun, I bought them Flintstones sleeping bags, and they loved them. We put the sleeping bags in a closet during the day (when I was organized enough to do so) and brought them out at night. Even in a small apartment they had their special, snugly sleeping bags—something of their own.

Wherever your children sleep, try to give them choices. Let them pick blankets for the bed or curtains for the window. If possible, let them decide where the furniture goes, help them put the room together their way, and have fun doing it together. Remember, it doesn't have to be done "right." Their space is their space—not yours. Allow them to personalize things so they feel comfortable.

Make sure that younger kids have a play area (their bedroom, the living room, or wherever) and older children have a study space. Let them decide with you where that will be. If you live in a place that allows it, consider a pet. If a dog or cat is too much, try a couple of fish, a gerbil, a hamster, or even a hermit crab.

If your children draw or write in school, with you, or other places, put their works of art and great literature on your refrigerator. Let them see those reminders that this is their home. Let them know that you are proud of what they do.

Consider having some things in their space from their mother's home. They may want pictures of their friends, their mother, themselves, you, or even their pet. Pictures of your children's mom may be difficult for you to have around, so with very young children you can choose which pictures—if any—to have. If slightly older children and teens want to put up pictures of their mom, let them know it is a bit hard for you to look at those pictures right now. See if you can both agree to locate them in certain places, put them away at certain times, keep the pictures out of the house for a while longer, or use other pictures.

Emotional Setup

Look at your home's emotional setup, the way your home feels to your kids. Is it a place of calm interactions, equal treatment, open communication, clear expectations, fair rules, reasonable chores, fun times, and respect for all people? Probably not all the time (mine wasn't always), but strive for that goal. Make your home as emotionally comfortable as you can. Keep your eyes—and your mind—open for ways to create a comfortable feel in your home.

Much of the feel of a house comes from how well parents handle household activities. I present brief thoughts here on chores, behavior, homework, mealtime, bedtime, and friendships, and I encourage you to seek more complete information in parenting books if you wish. The better you handle household activities, the more you and your children will enjoy being with each other.

As you deal with your children, remember that they spend most of their time in a home that probably has very different expectations about their activities and responsibilities. Be careful not to demand behavior in your home that is far from what's expected in their mother's. If you become too critical or angry with them, you take the joy out of being together.

It is, of course, important that you have expectations of your children when they are with you, but understand that children cannot easily change their behavior back and forth each time they go from one home to the other. I'm not saying you must raise them like their mother does. I only suggest that you look at the reality that they live in two different households, and take that into account when dealing with them.

Chores

When your live-away children stay with you, get them involved in deciding which chores they will do, and they will be more committed to completing them. Don't do your children's chores for them, but help younger children with theirs, and make them fun. If you are going to be doing them together, you might as well enjoy it.

Assign chores that can be done in a reasonable amount of time. Do your best to see that your children, stepchildren, and new children are treated fairly. Give a reward for successful completion of chores, such as play time together, allowance, or enthusiastic praise. Be careful not to criticize your child's work harshly, and if you point out a chore that needs to be done better, *always* make sure that you also point out what was done well.

Behavior

It's not always easy for kids to behave, and getting them to behave isn't always easy for adults, but you add to your chances of success by having realistic expectations of your children and being calm but firm in setting limits. Intervene early when they start to misbehave. Take into account their moods and needs, and remember that things that seem minor to adults are often very important to kids. Don't have many rules, but calmly and patiently stick to the ones you do have.

Accentuating the positive

When you must correct your children, *always also point out what they do well*. Noticing what they do correctly and pointing it out makes them believe in themselves and want to do it again.

Don't say this: "Jimmy! You call this cleaning your room? You still haven't made your bed. What's wrong with you? How many times do I have to tell you? Make your bed!"

Say this: "Well, Jimmy, you did a really good job of picking up your clothes, but you forgot to make your bed. Nice job on the clothes. As soon as you make the bed you'll be all done with chores for today."

Don't say this: "Roberta, you've done it again. You've been screaming all over the place. Stop making so much noise!"

Do say this: "Roberta, you are really good at being quiet sometimes. You have been getting too loud now though, and I'd really appreciate it if you would get back to that nice quiet playing you do so well. Thanks."

Direct involvement

Direct involvement with kids is very helpful. Children don't respond well from a distance. There are many times that you must get up, go to them, and redirect their behavior. Be sure you do this calmly, however, or they'll react to your anger rather than your guidance and redirection. Gently take younger children by the hand, or put your arm around the shoulder of older kids, as you calmly state in one or two sentences what you want them to do, and stay with them as they get started on that new activity.

Distraction

Distraction is another great parenting technique. You don't have to punish children for them to learn a lesson; simply distract them before their behavior becomes a problem. Distraction is particularly effective with children between the ages of about two and eight.

If you want your children to stop a certain behavior, distract them in a fun way. Get them involved in something else, and be *extremely energetic* about it. Point and gesture like crazy as you excitedly talk about, and point at, different things in their view. It doesn't matter what you point at or what you say. Make it up as you go along. The important thing is to totally distract them. Get them off their upset train of thought with great enthusiasm, and in two minutes they will follow you anywhere. Once you've got them hooked on you, move them onto another activity.

Homework

Show an interest in your children's homework and school in general. Do your best to communicate with their mother on this, and support her in expecting good school performance. Give your kids a quiet place to do homework regularly, set up a fixed time for it if possible, and look for ways to praise their effort.

Because the time you have with your children is limited, it can be extremely difficult to fit homework in, but do your best. Consider having them do it earlier in your time with them so it doesn't get put off to the last minute and really become a hassle.

Mealtime

Mealtimes can be tough for families. In many households they become power struggles between parents and children, and when that happens both sides lose. Children generally need to eat what's being served, but recognize that forcing them to eat your way will only make things worse. Instead of power struggles, give your children choices, and do so without anger.

Choices could include things such as eating her food nicely like everyone else or eating alone in the other room (not the child's room, if that's where she'd prefer to be). If your child is playing with her food or fooling around, let her know that is not acceptable behavior at the table. Tell her once—in a calm voice—that any further behavior like that will mean that she has chosen to not complete her meal (if you can't stand the idea of her going without food until the next meal, you may decide to allow her a snack in a couple of hours).

You can assume that your kids will test you to see if you mean what you say. It is crucial that you calmly follow through. Let the misbehaving child know her meal is over, take the food away, ask her to leave the room so the rest of the family can eat, and let her

know sincerely that you look forward to her joining you at the next
meal.

Don't get caught up in arguments or her requests to be for-
given. She knows the rules, and by deciding not to abide by them,
she's chosen to eat later or elsewhere (you decide which, that's not
her choice). Don't get angry at her either. Instead, calmly express
your fear that she will have an unhappy time until she does eat
or be sincerely sorry that she made an unwise choice to miss that
meal. When the next meal comes, be sure not to lecture her or remind her of her faults, just enjoy the meal.

Bedtime

Bedtime (in some families it's pronounced "bedlam") is something
that most children struggle with at one time or another. If your
home experiences difficult bedtime behavior, know that you are
not alone. Almost any reactions that occur around bedtime in your
place have happened in other people's families.

Kids often like the predictability of knowing what they will do
each evening, particularly if they are sleeping away from their
live-in home, so handle bedtime the same every night. A typical
routine might be something like this: pajamas on at 7:30 P.M.,
brush teeth, use the bathroom and get a drink of water by
7:45 P.M., read a story together until 8:00 P.M., and then you leave
the room.

Allow lights on and doors open if your children want it. Let
your kids read or play quietly in their bed before they fall asleep. If
children keep each other awake, try different bedtimes for children
according to their age, or try to put them to bed in separate rooms.
It also helps to speak with other parents and see what works for
them. They may have good suggestions.

Friendships

Choosing good friends doesn't come automatically to all children.
If you are concerned about the friends your children pick, you can

set limits on who your children bring into your home, but you can't effectively stop your kids from hanging out with them away from your place. I've seen parents try to make their kids stay away from certain friends, but the result was that those parents became angry investigators constantly hunting for proof of what their kids were doing, and their children became sneaky and disobedient.

The more you tell your kids that their friends are bad, the more they'll want to be with them. Instead of doing that, let your kids know you believe in their ability to make good decisions, and allow them to learn from their own mistakes.

Rather than set unenforceable limits, talk with your kids about their friends (don't lecture!). Listen to what they say. When you hear about their friends making poor decisions, briefly talk with your children about them, but don't try to convince them you are right, and don't expect them to agree. Just lay it out there, and let it go.

As a live-away dad you have a great opportunity to parent your children the way you think is best. Remember that giving them a couple of choices works better than forcing them to be your way. You get closest to your children when you listen to them, keep your comments brief, remain calm, and let them know you trust them.

Fun Stuff to Do

Looking for things to do with your kids? You're not alone. We all get stuck at times trying to figure out what to do on a cold January evening, a rainy Saturday, or a sunny Sunday for that matter. So I've drawn up a list of suggestions and present it here. I've arranged these activities by age, but it will be obvious that many of these things can be done at several ages.

It helps to plan ahead too. Don't wait until your twin six-year-olds are running laps around your knees before you start to think about what you're going to do with them that day. Think of things to do before your children arrive, or have special "planning meetings" with them each time they get there to see what all of you would like to do in your time together.

The following suggestions are only the tip of the creative iceberg. You have a lot more ideas inside you. Try mine when you get stuck, and come up with your own. When you generate ideas, be creative, loosen up, and most important have fun! Make sure you do more than just think about these activities—do them. Get active with your kids if you want to enjoy your time together. When you really get stuck for what to do, ask a play expert—your kid!

BIRTH TO ONE YEAR OLD:
Make faces at each other.
Have your child grip your finger with his hand.
Blow very lightly on her face.
Very gently and slowly stretch his arms to his sides.
Make googlie sounds and watch the smiles.
Massage her feet and hands.
Sing softly to him.
Watch his eyes move in response to you.

TWO TO THREE YEARS OLD:
Make more faces.
Play peek-a-boo.
Play in the bathtub.
Take her to the store with you.
Read picture books.
Play patty-cake.
Crawl around on the floor together.
Pound on boxes.
Hide in boxes.
Mimic sounds back and forth.
Roll a ball back and forth.
Play in the sand.
Go on a picnic together.

FOUR TO SEVEN YEARS OLD:
Bounce a ball together.

Have him nap in your arms.
Make up silly words.
Sing funny songs.
Make things out of cardboard boxes.
Draw or paint pictures.
Play hide-and-seek.
Build sand castles at the beach.
Read story or picture books to each other.
Play "go to work."
Make a book that tells a story with pictures.

EIGHT TO TEN YEARS OLD:
Play an instrument.
Read a book together.
Play crazy eights.
"Paint" temporary pictures on the sidewalk with a big brush
    and water.
Make a tent out of a sheet over a table.
Go for a walk.
Look at insects.
Play basketball with a crumpled-up piece of paper and a
    wastebasket.
Take her to work with you.
Go to the park.
Make a written secret code together.
Build a bookcase together.
Play a board game.
Play house.
Make up stories.
Make a book about school/a hobby/animals/winter/friends/the
    sun.
Play chef/doctor/mechanic/businessperson/pilot/astronaut/
    teacher.
Practice whistling.
Collect baseball cards.

ELEVEN TO THIRTEEN YEARS OLD:
Build a model together.
Ride bikes.
Make a birthday card for someone.
Look up words in the dictionary or play the dictionary game.
Go for a swim.
Go camping.
Build a fort together.
Tell scary stories.
Tell loving stories.
Talk about what you did as a kid.
Cook a meal together.
Volunteer for the elderly.
Play sports.
Draw spacemen.
Make up your own language.
Make a night game with flashlights.

FOURTEEN YEARS OLD AND UP:
Snow ski.
Water ski.
Talk about the future.
Go to a concert together.
Hunt.
Fish.
Bowl.
Play checkers or chess.
Take a long hike.
Listen to her stories about school.
Explore the Internet together.
Just the two of you go to a restaurant once a month.
Go to a Fourth of July fireworks display.
Attend a movie together.
Shop together for clothes/sports equipment/school
    supplies/books.

Bake a pie.

Plan and take a trip together.

Game Rules

Some live-away dads have difficulty playing with their children because of the bad blood between them and their children's mothers. It's hard to have fun when there is so much stress and tension. But some dads living with their kids seem to have trouble playing too. We become too goal oriented. Even when we play with our kids we want to produce a result, win the game, build a car model that looks great, do it the "right" way, play by the rules.

Not surprisingly, play that is too structured can interfere with having fun, so when playing games with your children please pay attention to *The One and Only Very Important Number One Game Rule*:

1. Stop having so many rules! That's the number one rule. Rules can really be a drag when you are trying to have fun. Don't get mad if your children want to change the rules in the middle of the game. Let them. Play with them. It's only a game. Teens may want to play by rules a lot of the time, but many kids often prefer to forget the rules or make up their own. Young kids just love to win, and they'll work hard to arrange any possible way to do so.

We live by rules so often at work and other parts of our adult lives that we forget to be spontaneous. If your child wants to make up her own illogical rules to a board game or card game, let her!

It's not only okay for your kids to make up their own rules in games, it's also fine for them to cheat. The idea of playing without rules and allowing kids to cheat is a tough one for most parents. We fear that allowing our kids to do that teaches them to cheat in other parts of their life now and as adults. But that is simply not so.

It would take too long to go into the reasons that some children and adults *do* cheat in life, but I can guarantee you that it's not because they played games with their dad in which they were allowed to do what they wanted. You have plenty of opportunities to teach your child about fair play and honesty in life, and those qualities are extremely important, but it is also important to sometimes be silly, laugh, and forget about doing things the "right" way. Many times, the best way to do that is forget the rules and just let go.

If it's hard for you to play without rules or allow your child to cheat, ask everybody playing the game if they want to have it be a "no rules" game where anything goes, including cheating. Then you will be playing by the rules when you don't have any rules. Don't be surprised, however, if you have more fun in those games than other games and your kids want to play "no rules" games all the time.

Playing is supposed to be fun! And I don't mean just intellectual fun and polite banter (although that certainly has its place). I mean hand-slapping, eye-watering, burst-out-laughing, forget-what-you're-doing, pee-in-your-pants, doesn't-matter-who-wins silliness! If your separation is new or there are other problems weighing you down, it's not easy to have fun. But it's a great goal. Allow yourself to let go when you can—both for your sake and your child's. Take humor seriously (Ha!).

Fun is an important and intimate part of any relationship. Fun times create memories and bring you and your children closer together. How many memories do you have of joking around and really having great fun with your father when you were a kid? If you have many, I'm sure you appreciate them. If you don't, do fun things with your kids now so they'll have those memories in their lives.

Make the Most of Your Time with Your Kids

When your children spend time with you, be sure you get actively involved with them. If your children are bored, don't just tell them to go play. Play with them whenever possible. Help them come up with ideas. Make a game out of coming up with ideas. See who can come up with the most interesting ones. Get creative. Get energized. Get involved.

When your kids aren't with you, your free time is your own. When your kids are with you, it's important to consciously switch gears and connect intimately with them. Certainly you have other responsibilities in your life, but take time for your kids. That's one of the challenges of being a live-away dad.

Another challenge is trying to play with your kids when they don't want to play. That can be frustrating. Especially if you are tired or stressed, it's easy for you to fall into patterns in which you read the paper, watch TV, do office work, or spend time on the computer while your kids play with each other or the other computer. Don't let that happen a lot.

The key to getting your kids involved with you is coming to them with energy and excitement. Get your energy level up. Become enthusiastic and excited. Whatever you do, have it in your head that you are going to do something fun together, and don't give up until you've got some enjoyable activity going.

When it comes to time with your children, don't just be a human *being*, be a human *doing*. Whether playing, working, doing chores, completing homework, eating, riding to the store, or talking on the phone, the quality of your relationship with your kids will reflect the energy you put into it. You don't have to be a one-man entertainment committee, but kids are little people, and those little people want to be with big people who take time for them, listen to them, and treat them well.

Get Involved in Your Child's Activities

Here are ways to be involved with your children in activities they might already be in. Do some of these, and come up with your own creative ways to increase your involvement with them.

Coach a team your child is on.
Volunteer in your child's classroom.
Be a chaperone on school field trips.
Become a scout leader in your child's troop.

Drive your child in the school car pool.

Transport your children when they apply for jobs.

Take your child clothes shopping.

Go shopping for school supplies at the beginning of the year.

Attend as many of their school events as you can (plays, sports, music concerts).

Volunteer at organizations your child is in such as the YMCA, YWCA, and FFA.

Drive them to summer camp, and pick them up at the end.

Be a Sunday school teacher in your child's class.

Help your child correspond with a pen pal.

Volunteer at your child's community play.

Teach your child to drive.

Attend music concerts together.

Go with them to tour college campuses they might attend.

Sad Dads, Mad Dads, and Glad Dads

Sad dads

Sad dads are often tired. Sometimes they let their kids get away with too much, because they don't have the energy to stop them. They often don't follow through with things they said they'd do. It's difficult for them to enjoy their kids. They sometimes feel like giving up. Their kids play in the other room a lot. Sad dads snap at the littlest things sometimes. They frown a lot.

Mad dads

Mad dads get angry easily. They don't talk much and when they do they tend to raise their voices or lecture. They complain about their children's mothers quite a bit—sometimes they even do it right in front of the kids or allow themselves to be overheard while talking on the phone. Mad dads tend to have a lot of rules. They can't stand noise or disruption. They snap at the littlest things sometimes. They don't get down on their hands and knees and play with their little kids. They are very serious.

Glad dads

Glad dads make time to play with their kids. They horse around with them. They use a lot of praise. They find good things to say about their children's mothers. They go out of their way to include their children in things they do. They frequently tell their kids what they do well (even the littlest things sometimes). They read stories. They listen patiently. They're fun to be with.

Which are you?

I've sketched three types of dads to help you see what your behavior may be like at times—and how it comes off to others. All of us have parts of the sad dad, mad dad, and glad dad in us. It's how often, and how strongly, we express them that matters.

Ask yourself how much time you spend in each mood around your children. Sit back and remember your specific behavior the last three or four times you were with them.

If you discover that you aren't often enough a glad dad, make it your goal. You may not reach that goal instantly, but do small things to be more glad with your kids. Make a commitment to do some of those things next time your kids are with you. Don't get down on yourself if you spend more time than you want being sad or mad, but work toward being more of a glad dad.

Be Positive and Patient

If I could change only two specific parenting traits that dads use with their children, I would have them be more positive and more patient. A lot of men that I've known personally and professionally

bring a particular strength to parenting, the ability to set firm limits with their children and stick to them. The down side of this
tremendous strength, however, is that some dads become too harsh
with their kids and lose sight of the need to have those limits enforced positively and with patience.

Be positive

Many dads teach their children by showing them what they do
wrong rather than what they do right. That's often how their dads
taught them. Those dads mean very well. It seems to make perfect
sense to point out errors so they won't be repeated. But the result
for children is constant reminders of what they do wrong. That decreases self-confidence.

Think about it. What child (or adult) wants to hear what they
did wrong all the time? What kid benefits from being with someone who constantly points out his mistakes?

If you find that you too frequently tell your children what
they've done wrong, stop and think a minute about how you were
raised. Do you remember the people who raised you praising you a
lot? Did they frequently tell you what you did well? Chances are
that your current parenting techniques are greatly influenced by
how these people handled you.

When I have this discussion with fathers (which is pretty often), some say things to me like, "So what if my old man told me
what I did wrong a lot? I learned, didn't I? At least I didn't end up
as wild as the kids today. I respect rules. It didn't hurt me a bit." I
understand those thoughts, but I must add that fathers can teach
their children to obey laws and respect adults even *more* successfully *without* constantly pointing out errors.

Believe it or not, kids usually have a pretty good idea of what
they do wrong anyway (though they aren't likely to admit their errors to someone who's constantly focusing on mistakes already).
A gentle reminder or reasonable consequence for errors will be
enough to help them get your message, and if you really want them

to listen to you, make sure you also tell them what they did well.

Children (even teenagers) are inexperienced in the world. There are many gaps in their understanding of themselves and of life in general, and our feedback is often what fills in these gaps. Filling those gaps with positive examples of what your children do well is more powerful and productive than filling them with mistakes they've made.

If you want your children to respect rules, like themselves, and be fun to have around, pay attention to whether you are negative with them. If you think you are too critical, work on stopping the negative statements. Find ways to point out what your children do well. You can still set limits, but do so without the negativity. Calm and consistent setting of limits creates desired behavioral change—negativity creates resistance.

Be patient

One way that dads are too impatient is in demanding immediate compliance from their children. It's necessary to stick to limits you've set but not to stand over your children with an angry face demanding instant results. That just sets up power struggles.

Let's look at an example of your son having the chore of taking out the garbage when the bag gets full. If he doesn't do his chore as required, you can respond with poor follow-through, impatient follow-through, or consistent and calm follow-through.

Poor follow-through means telling him to do it over and over without success—until you finally give up and take it out yourself. Impatient follow-through shows itself as angry words, occasional name-calling, and an angry physical stance to force him to do it right now (often after numerous "warnings" to do it). On the other hand, consistent and calm follow-through means telling him that he'll be free to watch television (use the phone, play with his friends, or some other activity) as soon as the garbage is taken out and enforcing that consequence without anger or negativity.

Another example might be a rule that your daughter put her

bike in the garage every night. Poor follow-through shows itself as ignoring the put-away-your-bike rule. Impatient follow-through means yelling and demanding instant compliance.

Instead of these approaches, let the consequences speak for themselves. Tell your daughter that you'll be glad to allow her to eat supper (go with her friends, play video games, etc.) as soon as her bike is put away. No demands for instant response. No yelling, anger, or emotional distance on your part. Instead, briefly express your fear about how she will deal with the consequences of her actions or your empathy about what she is missing by making the choice she did. Let the consequences speak for themselves while you continue to be a positive, patient dad.

There will, of course, be times that your kids will be angry with you and times when you will not like what they do (your infant cries for hours with colic, your five-year-old has a temper tantrum at church, your twelve-year-old picks on his sister, or your sixteen-year-old cracks up your car), but you can still love them even when you don't particularly like their actions. Very few parents (none?) are always positive and patient, but the more time you spend that way, the greater the likelihood that your children will respect you, learn from you, and want to be with you.

PART V

Building a Network
of Support

*You deserve a network of support that allows you to feel good
about yourself and make healthy decisions about your
children. Some men are reluctant to seek assistance for
personal struggles. They were raised to solve their problems on
their own. They even view support from others as a sign of
weakness. But getting support is not weakness—it's
strength.*

*The most successful and intelligent men in the world have
struggled with their emotions at times. While self-reliance
is admirable, few self-made men really did it alone. Most
great men had people behind them, people who may not
have made it into the history books but who were there
giving counsel, suggesting alternatives, and listening.*

*It is a wise man who uses all resources available to him to
overcome logical and emotional challenges. Effective problem
solving requires it. The man who recognizes and responds to
his emotional needs along with his intellectual needs puts no
limits on his own greatness and his child's.*

CHAPTER 13

Support and Counseling Options Explained

"There can be no proper interpretation of yourself to others if you are confused about yourself. . . . The first job is to get some clarity of understanding about yourself, what you are, and where you are going."
—HARRY D. GIDEONESE

You are never alone. There are many people—friends, family, other live-away dads; and professional therapists—who will support you. Don't hesitate to seek out their assistance. For most of us, it takes courage to go to a counselor, walk into a room full of men for a group meeting, or consider psychiatric medication. Many times we do so only after our situation has become almost intolerable, and that's unfortunate, because assistance from others can give us and our children many benefits, as well as improve our chances in court.

Under ideal circumstances, friends and family provide us with all the encouragement, ideas, listening, fathering suggestions, and emotional support that we need. Unfortunately, some of us don't have family or friends living nearby who support us in those ways, and, even when we do, we feel awkward going to them too often. If your friends and family aren't quite the right fit, other fathers or professional counselors can help.

In the five years during which I conducted custody studies and parenting-time mediation for the county court, many of the parents I worked with sought individual counseling outside the mediation sessions. In several cases I recommended it to mad moms who interfered with their children's time with their fathers, frustrated fathers who made unrealistic demands of their children's moms, or passive parents who were depressed and unassertive.

If you are currently involved in counseling or other professional support, I encourage you to stay with it. If you are considering such assistance, I encourage you to give it a try. If you worry that your child's mom may attempt to use it against you, I can assure you that in my experience professionals saw counseling as a sign of strength, not weakness.

What Do Titles and Degrees of Professional Counselors Mean?

This section provides an overview of the educational backgrounds and primary responsibilities of psychiatrists, psychologists, and therapists. It will help you make better decisions if seeking counseling. Because educational requirements and professional practices may vary a bit from state to state, consider this information a guideline rather than an exact standard.

Most mental-health treatment (also described as counseling, therapy, or psychotherapy, regardless of who does it) that is reimbursed by insurance is done by psychiatrists, psychologists, or therapists who hold master's degrees. Individuals with bachelor's degrees or less education are not likely to be recognized by courts or paid by insurance companies.

Those who spend the longest time in school and training are psychiatrists. A psychiatrist is a medical doctor (M.D.) whose education includes four years of college earning a bachelor's degree, followed by four years in medical school. They then receive four or five additional years of training as interns and residents in psychiatric settings.

As medical doctors, psychiatrists are able to prescribe medication for patients (clients). The primary work of many psychiatrists is to diagnose an individual's condition, prescribe and monitor medication for that person if they determine it is needed, and oversee therapy done by counselors with those patients. Most psychiatrists have been taught primarily about the human body and how medications interact with it and have received less education and training in counseling and psychotherapy techniques than the psychologists and therapists with master's degrees. Although some psychiatrists provide mental-health therapy for clients, many leave the ongoing counseling to psychologists and therapists while they see the client for medication management for fifteen to thirty minutes every two weeks to three months.

Most psychologists are also doctors but have their doctorate in psychology (Ph.D. or Psy.D). Some psychologists have a master's degree in psychology (M.A.). Master's-level psychologists cannot prescribe medication, but some Ph.Ds and Psy.Ds can to a limited extent. Psychologists with doctorates generally receive three to four years of education beyond their bachelor's degrees including a year of full-time supervised experience in a psychiatric hospital or other mental-health facility. Depending upon the setting in which they work, they may do psychological testing, case supervision, or counseling.

The majority of mental-health counseling in this country is done by individuals with master's degrees. Master's-level counselors undergo approximately two to three years of education beyond a bachelor's degree, which usually includes extensive supervised counseling experience. Master's-level therapists have degrees in social work (M.S.W.), educational psychology (M.Ed.), counseling (M.A.), or other fields with an emphasis in counseling. Master's-level professionals may go by many titles, but common ones are psychotherapist, therapist, counselor, clinical therapist, mental health therapist, and psychiatric social worker. Titles can vary, so do not hesitate to ask any of these professionals what their titles and credentials mean.

Nine Alternatives for Help

The following options for handling your separation more effectively are listed, more or less, in order from least to most intensive.
This doesn't mean any are "better" than others, they are just different, and it's up to you to decide which may be most helpful
for you.

Many men find it difficult to ask others for assistance, but the
benefits of doing so can be great. Do it for your children if not for
yourself, because if you handle situations better it helps them.
Think of it as a loan. Borrow some assistance now for your child's
sake, and pay it back by helping someone else out sometime in the
future.

Discussions with friends and relatives

Talks with friends and relatives can be very helpful. Those folks
may be a tremendous resource for you when you're trying to decide what to do in difficult situations—or just need someone to listen. Talking with others also brings us closer together, and that
closeness adds depth to our lives.

Self-help books

Self-help books can be a great source of information. I'll mention a
few here that I find helpful. There are many others, however, and I
encourage you to seek out books on any topics that interest you.
When clients in my private practice want more information on
specific subjects, I encourage them to find books by browsing the
self-help section of their local bookstore or looking in the library.
Here are some books I suggest:

Dinosaurs Divorce—A Guide for Changing Families
    Laurene Krasny Brown and Marc Brown
A cute book with big pictures that uses dinosaurs to explain divorce
to young children. Read this reassuring book with your children to

learn about exploring emotions, understanding what happened, and positive ways to handle parental separation. (32 pages) Little, Brown and Company

The Father's Almanac Revised
    S. Adams Sullivan
This excellent resource gives practical and specific advice on all sorts of parenting tasks, such as diapering, hygiene, discipline, play, bathing, and other activities in raising children up to the age of about six years old. (416 pages) Doubleday

101 Ways to Be a Special Dad
    Vicki Lansky
This playful little book suggests projects and activities you can do with your children under the age of about fourteen. (101 pages) Contemporary Books

The Five-Minute Lawyer's Guide to Divorce
    Michael Allan Cane
This attorney uses a question and answer format to give you extremely helpful information about all aspects of divorce, minus the attack-dog mentality of some divorce books. (304 pages) Dell Publishing

Parenting with Love and Logic: Teaching Children Responsibility
    Foster Cline, M.D., and Jim Fay
A book that, I believe, supports parenting in a more "masculine" style and emphasizes empathy rather than anger when interacting with children. Includes numerous "Parenting Pearls" on ways to handle specific situations such as stealing, sibling rivalry, mealtimes, etc. (227 pages) Pinon Press

P.E.T. Parent Effectiveness Training: The Tested New Way to Raise
    Responsible Children
    Dr. Thomas Gordan
A classic book on using "I-messages," active listening, "no-lose"

methods for resolving conflict, and other tools for communicating effectively with children. (332 pages) Plume Book/Penguin Putnam, Inc.

The Wounded Male: The First Practical, Hands-On Guide Designed to
   Help Men Heal Their Lives
   Steven Farmer
Through self-disclosure and intelligent insight, the author provides an opportunity for self-growth, including numerous rewarding exercises that might be most helpful for men with some experience in men's work and self-examination. (222 pages) Ballantine Books

The Anger Workbook
   Lorrainne Bilodeau, M.S.
Easy to understand and very helpful, this nonthreatening book on anger provides insight and exercises to help you deal with your anger. (114 pages) Hazelden

Feeling Good: The New Mood Therapy
   David D. Burns, M.D.
An excellent book for understanding and handling depression, hostility, and other strong emotions. (466 pages) Avon Books

Lectures and educational groups

Lectures and educational groups have two things in common. They are often free or cost very little, and they provide you with the opportunity to get information from professionals without lots of self-disclosure. There are a wide variety of topics you might find out more about, including child-rearing techniques, handling emotions effectively, relationships, surviving loss, anger, and legal considerations in divorce.

Presentations may be offered by churches, neighborhood centers, community organizations, hospitals, mental-health clinics, and social service agencies. You can find out about them in newspapers, through friends, from other live-away dads, on the radio, in agency brochures, on bulletin boards, or the Internet.

Support groups

I joined a men's divorce support group about six months after my marriage ended. Aside from my own determination, that experience was the single most influential reason that I stayed involved with my children after my divorce. I knew that I wanted to stay connected to my kids, but it was sometimes so painful, and there seemed to be so many obstacles in my way, that I can't be sure I would have done it without those other dads. I know I would not have done it as well.

Group members listened to me, encouraged me, and reminded me over and over again that my commitment to my daughters would pay off in the end if I stuck it out through the middle. I honestly didn't know at the time if they were right, but I stayed involved with my daughters hoping they were. Now I know they were.

Good groups are a place where people express the frustrations they're having and deal with problems they face with the ideas and assistance of other men going through the same thing. The guys there encourage each other as they begin feeling good enough about themselves to make the changes they need to in their lives.

Members get feedback on problems they struggle with and help others solve problems in return. Support groups respect individual differences and work to be sure that everybody feels included. Many are led by professionals experienced in group dynamics, but the members are considered the experts, and they decide what to talk about at each meeting.

Years after I had been a member of a support group for divorced dads, I began leading groups myself. I remember one man, Frank, who literally said little more than his name for the first four weeks he was with us. He was an intelligent and financially successful businessman with two teenage children he had only seen once in the ten months since his divorce. When he finally began to talk, Frank disclosed that he missed his kids tremendously but had seen them so little because contact with their mother was overwhelmingly painful to him.

Although his divorce was nearly a year old, Frank was still in shock. He had thought his was an excellent marriage right up to the moment his wife filed for divorce and moved out. She cleaned out their bank accounts, left with a coworker Frank knew, and took the kids. She had been planning it for months.

Frank was devastated by her departure, and now he was filled with guilt for not seeing his kids. He had signed up for two dads' divorce groups before this one but hadn't gone to either because he was afraid people would put him down for avoiding his children. It was only after weeks of experiencing the nonjudgmental attitude of other group members that Frank started to talk.

A few weeks after Frank started speaking up in group, he surprised everyone by telling us that he had contacted his kids and arranged a week's vacation together. He spent that week with his kids around the time of our eleventh meeting. It went beautifully. More and more, his painful thoughts about his children's mother were being replaced by pleasant thoughts about himself and his kids. It was great to see him coming out of his shell.

One of the most powerful things about a support group is that it lets people know they aren't the only ones with a problem. They hear stories that are remarkably similar to their own. This helps them feel understood and creates a common bond. Listening to other men talk about their own experiences allows guys to get rid of the shame that so often engulfs them.

For myself and many men I've known, another tremendous thing about support groups has been the lasting friendships that developed from them. Until I had been in men's support groups for quite a while, I had found it easier to talk to women than men. I had been raised primarily by and around women, worked mainly with women, and dated women. Becoming friends with men was not so easy. I needed regular, ongoing contact with men to make friends with them, and support groups gave me that.

I got to know my male buddies in high school through sports

and hanging out in school, but I rarely see them anymore. I made my college friends by living with them in the dorm, but I only talk to a few of them once or twice a year now. I've met great guys through jobs I've had, but for whatever reasons, none of them have become close friends with whom I spend time outside work.

Most of the male friends I have now are indirectly tied to that divorced dads support group I joined over eighteen years ago. After that group ended, some of those guys decided to start other activities for divorced dads, and I joined them. While volunteering with those men, friendships slowly developed.

After a few years, some of the guys I knew went through more intensive men's awareness experiences, and I got involved in that. Those groups led to more groups that I continue in today. I now have several male friends I can call when looking for someone to do things with or talk to, and that's really important to me.

Spiritual or religious guidance

Many people seek support and guidance through their place of worship or prefer to attend sessions with counselors who incorporate spiritual or religious beliefs into their counseling. These approaches can be powerful, particularly when those helpers have a professional counseling degree. The counseling skills, techniques, and supervised therapeutic experiences obtained through secular education combined with spiritual or philosophical views that fit with yours make that guidance very helpful indeed.

Individual counseling

A good therapist brings experience and training to the counseling session to help you make the changes you want to make in yourself. He works for you. How the therapist interacts with you, what theoretical basis he follows, and what methods he uses vary from one counselor to another. If you have any questions about the therapist's philosophy or technique, ask him what it is. If you are ever unsure of what he's doing or why he's doing it—ask him. If he doesn't give you clear answers, go somewhere else.

Studies have shown that no specific therapeutic method is particularly better or more successful than others. Change is usually more a result of your therapist's skill in using the approach he has chosen and your comfort level with him. If you feel that he understands you, has true concern for your growth, and makes sense in what he does with you, you are probably with a therapist who can help.

Confidentiality is an important part of any counseling relationship, and states provide strict regulations governing it. Although your conversations with a therapist are carefully protected, there may be situations in which court orders allow access to information disclosed in sessions. If you are concerned about the privacy of your conversations with a therapist, be sure to ask about confidentiality when you begin therapy.

Ultimately, your willingness to work on self-change is the single most important factor in getting better. Counseling is a powerful tool for people who are interested in changing themselves.

Medication

Many men are reluctant to take medicine because they don't like pills, they fear side effects, or they simply want to handle things on their own. I respect that thinking but also feel that medications are of great assistance to people who use them appropriately. There are medications available today that are often very effective in treating depression, anxiety, and anger problems.

As a custody evaluator and parenting-time mediator, I considered the use of doctor-prescribed medication to be positive. It certainly made more sense than having parents continue harmful behaviors around their children when responsible use of medication could improve things.

I suggest to my clients in private practice that they consider medication if we find that the counseling is not working, but because skills don't come in pills, I always encourage them to continue their involvement in therapy. Medications are helpful, but they don't teach us how to cope with stress, deal with our emotions, or express ourselves more assertively. Several months of medication treatment acts as a jump start to get us back on track, and counseling allows us to maintain that improvement after the medication is discontinued.

Alcohol and other drug-abuse treatment

Alcohol and other drug-abuse treatment usually begins with the individual stopping all use of alcohol or drugs. Treatment may be outpatient (usually seeing a counselor once or twice a week or every two weeks), day treatment (this option, which may be available for mental-health counseling as well, consists of several hours of individual and group counseling each day), or inpatient (living in the hospital while treatment is going on). Generally, the more severe the substance abuse, the more likely it is that inpatient care is needed.

Professional counseling is extremely important. For most people, thorough treatment requires more than Alcoholics Anonymous or related twelve-step programs. As important as those programs are, they are not the entire treatment, and I highly recommend additional professional counseling.

If you believe your child's mom has a problem with alcohol or drugs, try to get officials to investigate it, but be aware that they may not do so to your satisfaction. If allegations have been made against you, explore the situation further with a professional counselor, not because your child's mom wants you to, but because substance abuse, if present, robs you of a relationship with your children.

Inpatient mental-health treatment

When I conducted custody studies and parenting-time mediation and came across a parent who had received inpatient psychiatric hospitalization, I looked at several things when evaluating that parent and his hospitalization. I considered how many times he had received inpatient treatment, how long ago it was, what the circumstances leading up to it were, how he felt and talked about it, and how his emotional health has been over the last several years.

In battles over custody or parenting-time, parents sometimes tried to use prior hospitalization of the other parent as proof of how "crazy" he or she was, but as a court-appointed social worker, I didn't automatically see inpatient hospitalization as proof of anything. Repeated hospitalizations were of greater concern, but, as always, I looked at the many aspects of that parent's behavior when assessing parenting.

There are a variety of support options available to you that will enhance your growth as a dad—as well as your chances in court. To deal with your former partner and your children more effectively, take advantage of some of the resources I've presented here. I've talked to many dads who were initially reluctant to try any of them but found after doing so that they were much easier and far more helpful than they'd expected.

Of all the options I've presented here, a support group is the one I most often recommend to live-away dads. It's the least expensive and most beneficial resource of them all. I think support groups are so useful, and potentially so powerful, that I've made them the final chapter of this book. They could be the first chapter in a whole new life for you.

CHAPTER 14

Build Your Own Support Group

"No man is the whole of himself. His friends are the rest of him."
—*Good Life Almanac*

R eal" men do join support groups. Unfortunately, some people in this society have come to think that talking about
problems in groups is whining, but nothing could be further from the truth. Whining is endlessly complaining and making
excuses. A healthy support group is a place to express yourself honestly for the purpose of making positive life changes. There's nothing whiny about that.

I talked in previous chapters about the many benefits of support
groups: realizing that you aren't the only person in your situation,
hearing what's happening with other live-away dads, talking with
fathers who won't judge you, being with guys who understand
what you're going through, hearing how other dads overcome
problems, helping other fathers who are hurting, and adding new
friends to your life. Here is my definition of a support group:

A support group is a safe and confidential place to talk
openly and honestly about what's going on in your life, and
find solutions to problems or simply be heard, by nonjudgmental people who understand and support you.

Groups help you deal more effectively with stress, give you ideas about how to handle conflict that comes up, and provide a safe outlet for your frustrations. As a result of group attendance, many live-away dads deal with their former partners better, see their children more often, and more fully enjoy the time they have with their children.

How to Find a Support Group

To find a group, ask other dads if they know of any. Also contact public, private, religious, or nonsectarian social-service agencies in your area. Those could include your county social-service agency, family-court counseling center, public mental-health association, mediation services, Catholic Social Services, Lutheran Social Services, the United Way, or many others. If there is an information line, hot line, or stress line in your area, call them and ask.

Look for leads in the phone book under "divorce," "men," "fathers," "counseling," "social-service agencies," "mental health," or related topics. Search for groups on the Internet. If there are fathers' rights groups or other men's organizations, ask them if they know of support groups. Judges, court social workers, mental-health professionals, or your attorney may know of resources.

You are most likely to find support groups referred to as "divorce support groups," or "men's divorce groups," but they are probably open to live-away dads who were never married as well. Contact them and ask. Similar groups such as general issues men's groups, church groups, parenting groups, or anger management groups may be an option as a second choice, but they usually don't provide you with the opportunity you need to deal directly and fully with the specific and powerful issues that are so important to live-away dads.

Start Your Own Group

If you can't find a support group—start your own. This section of questions and answers gives you the basics you need to start and run a live-away dads support group.

How do I get started?

The first thing to do is get other live-away dads involved in helping you set things up, to be members of the group, or both. Ask any dads you know that don't live with their children. They could be coworkers, friends, or relatives. Put the word out. Let people know you're trying to start a group, and ask them to tell anyone they know. If you are aware of legal or social-service professionals who have contact with other live-away dads, tell them.

Advertise in church bulletins, put an ad in the newspaper, tell professionals at your EAP (Employee Assistance Program at work), use the Internet, or contact therapists who work with men. Put up flyers at union halls, your workplace, the courthouse, mental-health associations, public libraries, police departments, apartment buildings, or any other locations where live-away dads or their partners may see them.

Another approach is to contact the agencies and organizations mentioned earlier in this chapter. Even if they don't conduct groups themselves, they may have access to resources such as meeting space, facilitator training, or ideas about where to find other dads interested in a group. They also might have, or know of, a professional with an interest in serving as a volunteer to help you get started. If you find someone who is helpful, ask him if he will assist you further or if he knows anyone who might.

I'm not a professional. How can I run a group?

Very well, I'd say. Although I would suggest getting an experienced facilitator if possible. Because of your own emotional pain, you may need to be a group member for a while, not a leader. When you lead a group you have less opportunity to vent your own frustrations, and that may limit your effectiveness for others and personal growth for yourself.

If you haven't led at least a couple of different support groups in your life, you may not appreciate how challenging it can be at times. An experienced facilitator will help the group run more smoothly, even if he only leads or coleads several of the first meetings to show you how.

As challenging as it is to lead a group, you *can* do it if you are open-minded and willing to learn. If you decide to lead, look for any information you can find on support-group facilitating, and try to find training on leading support groups. Draw on your experience as a group member of other groups, or try a rotating leadership in which different members lead the group each week.

What is the leader's role in a support group?

The leader sets the tone of the group. Remembering how awkward men may feel the first few meetings, he goes out of his way to welcome new members and help them feel comfortable. His role is to guide—not control. The facilitator does his best to see that the discussion stays on track, that everyone gets a chance to speak, that group members do a lot more talking than he does, and that all members feel accepted.

There may be a lot of anger and sadness expressed in meetings. Men may shed tears and express great frustration or fear. This is the perfect place to do it. When it happens, just listen. Don't give advice, and gently stop other dads who try to do so. Lots of times all we want is a chance to talk. This is extremely powerful. Never underestimate it.

The facilitator does not have to be the expert with the answers ("I don't know. Does anyone else here have any ideas?"). He doesn't determine what gets talked about or solve other people's problems—members are responsible for solving their own problems. He is not solely responsible for the success of the group—all members share in that.

Aren't these meetings really just gripe sessions?

Not if you want them to last! Gripe sessions are different from meetings in which people legitimately vent their feelings and resolve problems. But there is a danger that groups will become bogged down with complaints, and the group leader's ability to redirect negativity is an essential ingredient for group success.

Gripe sessions are a bunch of strangers sitting alone in a room. Healthy support groups are a collection of people supporting each other.

Gripe sessions are meetings in which dads (or the participants of any group) cut down other people. Healthy support groups allow people to vent strong feelings but also encourage self-responsibility.

Gripe sessions encourage complaints about others. Healthy support groups encourage men to talk about themselves.

Gripe sessions give members the feeling that some people—even other members of the group—aren't really that important. Healthy support groups convey respect for the needs and importance of all people and make it clear to each and every person there that he is an important part of the group.

Gripe sessions feed on anger. Healthy support groups allow for the expression of anger but get energy from growth beyond it.

Gripe sessions constantly rehash stories of the bad things that happened. Healthy support groups allow men to tell their stories of the past as they encourage them to rewrite their future.

Gripe sessions are constantly negative, and people leave them feeling angry and drained. Healthy support groups give people a chance to be heard and understood, and participants leave them feeling optimistic and energized.

Should it be men only?

I suggest male-only groups for live-away dads. Mixed groups can work well and may be necessary in areas where there are not enough fathers to keep a group going, but the presence of women in groups does change things. Many men and women tend to subconsciously alter what they say when the opposite sex is present. Members may feel less free in expressing negative emotions toward the other sex, and men may be reluctant to swear, get loud, or generally act the way they would with just guys in the room.

When men and women are present, members may find themselves competing for attention and even getting romantically involved. That can become a problem for vulnerable adults who may be better off staying out of relationships for a while, and it completely changes the dynamics of the group. Simply put, the addition of women to live-away dad support groups may work very well, but it also has the potential to create competition and pairing-up that could distract from the purpose of the group.

How many fathers are needed for a successful group?

A good number for live-away dad groups is about six or eight fathers. As few as three or four members may be enough, but when you get more than eight guys or so, the time available for each man to be heard decreases, and with the intensity of emotions that exist in such groups, time to speak is very important. Still, the divorced dads support group I was in had about fifteen members. It was a large group but a great help to me, and I'd rather be in a large group like that than turn men away.

Where can we meet?

Finding a place to meet is easy, and you can usually find one that is free or almost free. Consider space in a social-service agency, community center, church, or your home. You can also try alternating the meeting location between the homes of interested members. Meeting outside your home lends a bit of stability to what you are doing (the group can meet when you are sick or on vacation), and some fathers may feel more comfortable in a more "professional" setting. On the other hand, meeting in a home may be seen as more "neutral" than a church setting, for example, and some dads might like the informality.

What should the meeting room be like?

As far as the space itself is concerned, there is little needed other than a room big enough to comfortably fit the number of men in attendance. It is important, however, that it be relatively quiet and free from outside interruptions. Wherever you meet, try to see that no other people can hear you. Dads may be inhibited if they think their words will be heard by people outside the group.

What is a good length for meetings?

Meeting length might be something the group would like to decide, but one and a half or two hours is a typical length. Always start and end meetings on time. That discourages men from coming late and respects the need of members to get to other things after the meetings.

How often should we meet?

I recommend that groups meet weekly. This allows dads a chance to get to know each other more quickly. Some types of groups meet every two weeks or even once a month, but usually that is not often enough for live-away dad groups in which needs are so intense.

For men to feel comfortable with each other, they need trust and time. Trust develops when participants stick to the group guidelines and create an atmosphere that is confidential, respectful, and positive. If the group promotes trust, then time and frequent exposure to each other is all that's needed for dads to benefit.

How many times do we need to meet?

Limited-length groups are scheduled to run a certain number of weeks (usually eight, ten, or twelve) and stop. Other groups are open-ended. In limited-length groups, names are usually collected on a waiting list until enough men are available, then all men start and end together. In open-ended groups, there is no end date, and men join any time they want. In my opinion, open-ended groups are best because they are immediately available and dads can continue to benefit from them for a long time.

It may take a while for men to become comfortable in the group, so I recommend that they attend for at least four sessions or more of either group. Some dads remain in open-ended groups for a long time. For them, the group becomes like a healthy family they've chosen—a place where they can be heard, supported, and encouraged.

Is there a specific meeting format we can use?

There are many different structures or formats that could be used to run a group. I like a simple format and run a group in three parts. I start with a quick opening round, proceed to the middle of the meeting, and end with a very brief closing round. If you use this three-part format, each time a new man joins the group, give a quick overview of it at the beginning of group and a slightly more detailed explanation of each of the three parts as you enter them.

In the opening round, each dad, one at a time, tells how his week went and how he's feeling right now in group. The opening round is intended as a summary, so I often set a three- or five-minute time limit for each father. Without a time limit, some men tend to talk at great length.

The opening round helps men relax and gives them at least one chance to express themselves in the meeting. Hopefully they'll get an opportunity to speak more in the middle of the meeting, but some nights it's hard to give everybody all the time they need. If a dad is talking beyond his three or five minutes, ask if he'd like to talk about his subject in the middle of the meeting. If, as facilitator, you sense that a man has a lot to talk about but says it's not that important, your gut feeling is probably right. Encourage him to say more in the middle section of the meeting.

The middle of the meeting is the longest part. It is important that everyone who asks for time gets some here. In the middle portion of the meeting, dads talk back and forth (hopefully, one at a time), tell what's been happening in their life, express their feelings, ask questions, and get and give feedback.

Keep the focus mainly on the emotional struggles and everyday challenges of live-away fathering. You might spend time talking about legal strategies and what live-in moms have done, but redirect things if guys spend too much time on those subjects. Excessive complaints about people or the legal system can cause meetings to deteriorate into unproductive gripe sessions.

The closing round in groups I facilitate is usually one minute per man, and then the meeting is over. Be sure to start it soon enough to finish the meeting on time. One minute doesn't sound like much time, but it is usually enough for this summary. Consider having a timekeeper be responsible for holding dads to their time limits in closing rounds or the meeting may begin to drag, and you want it to end with energy.

Dads can talk about anything they want in the closing round but usually address one of three things. They sometimes expand upon or clarify something they said earlier. ("I just wanted to say that I really went off tonight about my son's mom, but I want you guys to know I feel calmer now and won't do anything stupid. I'm going to try to do as Matt said he's done with his ex. Thanks, Matt.") They may comment on how the meeting was for them. ("This was really a great meeting for me today. I feel a lot better.") They may express agreement or support. ("Hey, Charles, I just want you to know it was great to see you here this week, and I give you a lot of credit for keeping your cool with your kid's ma. Keep up the good work, man.") The closing round ties loose ends together and finishes the meeting on a positive note.

Group Guidelines

The following guidelines are appropriate for almost any support group. You may want to use these guidelines in yours or find others you are more comfortable with. Sometimes groups customize guidelines to fit their specific circumstances. Any time you have a new group member, briefly present the group guidelines and answer any questions he may have.

1. *Maintain confidentiality.* Whatever is said in group stays in group. For some groups this means nothing that happens in group can be talked about outside it. In other groups it means that members can tell outside people only what they said. This is the most important group guideline. Make sure that you define it clearly and that all members agree to maintain confidentiality before you proceed.

2. *Don't tell people what to do.* Instead, either ask permission to give someone feedback, or let that person know what's worked for you. Asking permission sounds like this: "Lucas, do you mind if I give you a suggestion?" Then Lucas might respond, "Yeah, Robert, go ahead" or "No, Robert, I just want to say this."

Tell group members what works for you. Instead of saying, "Jeez, Logan, I think you should tell your kids to go to their rooms when they get on your nerves," say what worked for you in the past, something like, "When I get mad at my kids, Logan, I just tell them to go to their rooms while I calm down. It helps me a lot."

3. *Talk one person at a time.* Give the speaker the respect of listening. Don't have side conversations going on. Encourage a lively discussion in which everybody talks back and forth—one at a time.

4. *Members may pass.* Although we invite and encourage people to talk, we allow them to do so at their own pace. No one is forced to talk. Let them gain from the group their way.

5. *Talk "to" group members, not "about" them.* Instead of saying to the group, "Man, Maynard seems awful mad about that," look at Maynard and say directly to him, "Man, Maynard, you look awful mad about this."

6. *Tell people what you think.* Don't hold back to be "nice," but don't go around blasting people either. Use the suggestions here to say things honestly and respectfully.

7. *Talk about feelings.* If a group member tells long stories of what happened, encourage him to talk about his feelings ("Hey, Graham, how did you feel when that happened?" or "Were you sad when she did that, Graham?"). Frankly, stories can get boring if they don't include feelings.

8. *Avoid excessive problem-solving.* Men, in particular, often want to "solve the problem" and may interrupt to give advice. Discourage this, and encourage men to listen instead.

9. *Resolve group conflicts.* Talk in your group about concerns or disagreements you have about what goes on in it, and remember that the purpose of speaking up is to promote trust while supporting all members of the group.

10. *Let people know before you leave the group.* This allows everybody a chance to understand what's going on with you and to say good-bye.

If you have an opportunity to join or start a group, I encourage you to take it. It may seem a bit intimidating at first, but I have been told by many live-away dads that they found it much easier and more helpful than they had expected.

SOME PARTING WORDS FOR DADS

Be in It for the Long Haul

There are few things more agonizing than separation from your children. There are few things more rewarding—and important—than being a part of their lives. Even from a distance, you have a tremendous influence.

Many live-away dads disconnect from their kids not because they don't love them—but because they love them too much. They struggle with their pain of separation in a court and social-service system that often both subtly and overtly favors women as parents. But you cannot let that system, your child's mother, or your own pain stop you!

For many dads, the first year or so after separation from their children and their children's mothers is the most difficult. It is vital that you seek support from other fathers during that time to establish a pattern of staying involved.

Put your children's needs first as you look carefully at your own actions. You can't go wrong if you do that. To put your children's needs first you must deal with your own hurt and frustration successfully by looking at yourself—not your children's mom or anyone else.

When the actions of your children's mom harms your kids, try to work cooperatively with her to change those actions. If you can't do that, consider court action, but, either way, think about what you can change and what you can't before you act. Make sure your desire to change her isn't driven by your anger, and see that your reactions are not more harmful to your children than her actions.

You have every right to be angry, frustrated, and hurt about this separation, and those powerful emotions can be difficult to handle. But you can channel them effectively. The reward for your effort includes a great relationship with your children and the opportunity to be a tremendous influence in their lives now and in the future.

You decide what happens in your life. You must realize how crucial you are to your children, even when they don't and their mother doesn't. She may appear to erect barriers to your fathering. Your children may not seem to appreciate what you do . . . yet. But your children will understand in time if you remain a committed, calm, and caring dad.

When your child was born, you started a journey together, a journey through childhood and adulthood. One that spans many years and has countless unforeseen turns. That has not changed. The path you have been on is not the one you expected, but it remains as important. It may seem like a different path from your child's. But it is not. The physical distance between your paths is not an impossible obstacle to a father who masters the emotional journey. Whether you walk hand in hand or many miles apart, you are traveling together.

Your journey began with the immensely intimate physical, emotional, and spiritual union between father and child. It will end in circumstances yet unknown. Your life will not turn out as you thought it would. It doesn't for anyone. But it will reflect how you live it. Stay positively involved in your child's life over the long haul.

INDEX

actions and acting:
  accepting responsibility for,
    17–18
  with anger, 26, 30–33
  with depression, 42–51
Alcoholics Anonymous, 209
alcoholism, 16
  communication and, 163–64
  court system and, 131, 133–34
  in depression, 42, 46
  finances and, 70
  in harm, 87
  in parenting-time evaluations,
    131, 133–34
  treatment for, 209
anger, 223
  acknowledgement of, 26–28
  acting differently with, 26, 30–33
  and allowing time to pass, 26, 33,
    51
  assessment of, 26, 28–30
  child-friendly homes and,
    175–76, 180, 182–85, 192–93,
    195–96
  childrens' mothers and, 57, 60,
    62–67
  communication and, 31–32, 96,
    98, 101, 106, 158, 168, 170–73
  counseling for, 200, 204, 208
  court system and, 112–13, 116,
    118–19, 121–22, 130, 132–33,
    135, 140–41, 146–52
  dealing with, 19–34
  in depression, 24, 34, 37, 39,

    41–42, 44, 46–47, 50
  excessive, 23–26
  finances and, 71–73
  harm and, 78–79, 81–82, 87,
    90–91
  physical, 21, 23
  physical symptoms of, 27
  Quadruple–A method for, 26–33
  in reacting to breakups, 9–10,
    13–18
  recognition of, 21–23
  stepfathers and, 68
  support groups for, 200, 204,
    208, 212, 214–15, 221
  verbal, 21–23
Anger Workbook, The (Bilodeau),
  204
apartments, *see* homes
appetite:
  communication and, 158
  in dealing with anger, 24
  in depression, 35–36, 41, 45
  in reacting to breakups, 7–8
  see also mealtimes
Aristotle, 20

baby–sitters, xix
behavior:
  in child-friendly homes, 176,
    180–84, 193, 195
  childrens' mothers and, 58
  in communication, 99, 106, 158,
    163
  court system and, 119, 123, 126,

support and counseling for, 203, 210

see also childrens' mothers; step-parents

parenting time and parenting-time mediation, xiii–xv, xvii–xix

answering questions fully in, 152–53

and childrens' mothers, 59–61, 64–65, 171–72

and communication, 98–99, 101, 103, 171–73

and court system, 111–13, 121–22, 128–54

emotions in, 131–32, 147–48

evaluating parenting abilities in, 130–33

extended time periods in, 137, 140, 144–46

and finances, 71–76

flexible vs. fixed schedules in, 136–39, 145–46

for grandparents, 101

and harm, 79–80, 87–88

holidays in, 137, 140, 142–44, 146

ongoing schedules in, 137, 139–43, 146

process of, 128–30

in reacting to breakups, 6

sticking to point in, 150

succeeding in, 136–54

and support and counseling, 199–200, 208–10

support of other parents' time with children in, 134–35

tips on, 146–54

voluntary, 136

Parenting with Love and Logic: Teaching Children Responsibility (Cline and Fay), 203

Peale, Norman Vincent, 95

P.E.T. Parent Effectiveness Training: The Tested New Way to Raise Responsible Children (Gordon), 203–4

Phil Donahue Show, 3

physical anger, 21, 23

positiveness, 224

in child-friendly homes, 181–82, 193–96

communication and, 99, 103, 106, 164, 170–71

court system and, 123

for depression, 47–51

in reacting to breakups, 18

in support groups, 208, 211, 220, 215

psychological evaluations, 127, 131

Quadruple-A method:

for anger, 26–33

for depression, 41–51

quick fixes, 93–94

reasonable visitation, 137

relaxation exercises, 44–45

reminders, 50–51

responsibility:

for actions, 17–18

communication and, 97, 99–100, 163, 167

court system and, 153

risk-taking, 46–48

Roosevelt, Eleanor, 121

runaways:

communication and, 169

harm and, 81–82

sad dads, 192–93

sarcasm, 21–22

schools, *see* education

seclusion, 36

234   *Index*

  in child-friendly homes, 194
  communication and, 167
  court system and, 121
  in dealing with anger, 23, 25–26
  with stepfathers, 68
self-esteem, 41, 44, 46, 71
self-help books, 202–4
self-talk, 28, 48
separations, *see* divorces
sex, communication on, 174
SHARE approach, 97–100
shared communication, 97–98, 100
siblings, xii–xiii
  in child abuse, xii
  in child-friendly homes, 179
  communication with, 95, 103–4
  in dealing with anger, 30
  harm and, 91
  in reacting to breakups, 12
  in support and counseling, 203
sleep and sleep problems:
  in child-friendly homes, 184
  and communication, 158
  in dealing with anger, 24
  in depression, 36, 41–42, 45
  in reacting to breakups, 9
socializing, 47–48
spiritual or religious guidance, 207
stepchildren:
  in child-friendly homes, 175–77, 181
  communication with, 95–97, 104–7
stepparents, xx
  in child-friendly homes, 175–76
  childrens' mothers and, 56–57, 67–69
  in reacting to breakups, 12
suicidal thoughts, 37–38, 41, 43
Sullivan, S. Adams, 203

support and support groups, 3–4, 9–10, 197, 199–221, 223
  building your own, 211–21
  definition of, 211
  discussions with friends and relatives in, 202, 207
  finding them, 212
  formats of, 218–20
  frequency of meetings of, 217–18
  as gripe sessions, 215, 219
  guidelines for, 220–21
  lengths of meetings of, 217–18
  locations of meetings of, 216–17
  male-only, 216
  number of members of, 216
  role of leaders of, 214–15
  running of, 213–14
  starting of, 213–20
see also counselors and counseling

taking care of yourself, 1
teachers, *see also* education
Ten Commandments of Communication, 60–66, 69
Three Deep Breaths, 44–45
two- to three-year-olds, fun things to do with, 186

underinvolvement, 10–11
Updike, John, 157

verbal anger, 21–23
violence, 3–4, 6
volunteer work, 33

Wang, An, 136
weight gain and loss, *see* appetite
Wounded Male: The First Practical, Hands-On Guide Designed to Help Men Heal Their Lives, The (Farmer), 204